THE DRIVING FORCE

Get Your Free Incredible Gift! Worth $747.83 — DrivingForceBook.com

MASSIVE BUSINESS GROWTH FORMULA

...Instead of the typical small, slow growth model everyone else is using

You Will Discover:

Why You Must Choose Massive Growth

How To Find Your Massive Idea

How To Get Into Massive Action Mode

The Power Of Connecting To Extraordinary People

The Importance Of Access To Extraordinary Resources

THE DRIVING FORCE MASTERMIND | WALTER BERGERON & SAM FRENTZAS

THE
DRIVING FORCE
Massive Business Growth Formula

How to grow your business with massive leaps instead of the small and slow growth models that everyone else is using.

Walter Bergeron
&
Sam Frentzas

Elite
Entrepreneur
Publishing

The Driving Force
Massive Business Growth Formula

Trademark ™ 2017 by Walter Bergeron LLC

All rights reserved. Copyright under Berne Copyright Convention, Universal Copyright Convention, and Pan-American Copyright Convention. No part of this book may be reproduced, stored in a retrieval system, or transmitted in any form, or by any means, electronic, mechanical, photocopying, recording or otherwise, without prior permission of the author.

ISBN-13: 978-1976504082

ISBN-10: 1976504082

Published by Elite Entrepreneur Publishing

Visit the Author Website:

www.TheDrivingForceBook.com

Disclaimer
While the authors have used their best efforts in preparing this book, they make no representations or warranties with respect to accuracy or completeness of the contents of this book. The advice and strategies contained herein may not be suitable for your situation. You should consult a professional where appropriate. The authors shall not be liable for any loss of profit or any other special, incidental, consequential, or other damages. The purchaser or reader of this publication assumes responsibility for the use of these materials and information. Adherence to all applicable laws and regulations, both advertising and all other aspects of doing business in the United States or any other jurisdiction, is the sole responsibility of the purchaser or reader.

Acknowledgements

<u>Walter Bergeron</u>

I really want to thank one of the people that has been there with me through thick and thin. She encouraged me when I needed to raise my spirits and kicked me in the butt when I needed to get to work and just get it done. The simple words of "thank you" don't express anywhere near enough gratitude for what she has endured to be with me for these two plus decades, but I want her to know that I do truly thank her for being one of the biggest reasons for my accomplishments. Thank you Jana.

Thank you Evan, for allowing me to be a father to an amazing son.

<u>Sam Frentzas</u>

Thank you to my brothers and sisters and my parents for being a family rich in relationships and love.
I am sure I have missed many people and they all deserve my deepest Thank you. I want to thank the people on this journey with me. When self-doubt crept in, that wasn't an option from the highs to the low's she's been my true north and My Driving Force. Thank you, Peggy.

Thank you, James, for being the son I dreamed of.

Leia, for being the biggest dreamer.

Thank you to my Sister and Brother and Mother who kicked me in the ass and patted me on the back along the way.

To my late father James Frentzas, my best friend the man who took down the path of being who I am today. You left me with two quotes that will never leave me, when I wanted to move to California at 18 you said no, you wanted to raise me you wanted "my handprint on your heart" I would not be the person I am today if I moved. You talked about legacy, if I become half the man you are then I leave this earth the richest man.

I can't name everyone I want to thank and they know who they are, Thank you.

About The Authors

Walter Bergeron

Walter Bergeron is a down to earth, blue-collar, multi-millionaire serial entrepreneur owning and operating as many as six companies simultaneously. Mr. Bergeron is a best-selling author and Marketer of the Year. This US Navy veteran started his entrepreneurial journey at the young age of 12, detailing automobiles in his parents' driveway. In 1996, after he completed a U.S. Navy tour aboard the nuclear-powered aircraft carrier USS Carl Vinson, he started his industrial repair company in a small shed in the middle of the sugarcane fields of Louisiana. His entrepreneurial path has led him to the latest sale of one of his companies for $10 Million. He is now guiding other driven blue-collar entrepreneurs on a path to exponentially grow their business to achieve their own eight figure lifestyle. For a free one on one personal business strategy session with Mr. Bergeron go to www.TheDrivingForceBook.com

About The Authors

Sam Frentzas

Sam Frentzas grew up in an Entrepreneurial family rooted in his father's belief that you must treat a customer well, and offer a quality product. Spending time with his family is his biggest driver to his continued success. This goes back to even when he was working at his father's clothing stores during the summers and while attending Loyola University. There Sam built a strong work ethic that carried over as a Commodity Trader at the Chicago Mercantile Exchange. During the span of a ten year trading career, Sam also graduated from the Conservatory Program at Second City, performing and writing many sketch comedy acts on stage. In 2005 Sam also became a member of the Screen Actors Guild, which he still belongs to today. Sam's real passion lies in being an entrepreneur. Then he earned the coveted position of Director of Sales for a financial information company, Sam saw the value in smart marketing and opened his own successful financial information company and takes real pride in helping other entrepreneurs reach their maximum potential. For a free one on one personal business strategy session with Mr. Frentzas go to www.TheDrivingForceBook.com

Contents

Acknowledgements

Introduction..v

Chapter 1
The Unvarnished Truth...................................1

The Unvarnished Truth	2
Entrepreneurs Need a Massive Growth Strategy	3
You'll Need Help From The Outside	4
One Is The Most Dangerous Number In Business	4
Connections To Extraordinary People	7
Private Information	8
Diverse Skills	9
Power Of Additional Connections	10
Connections To Extraordinary Resources	11
How To Read This Book	13

Chapter 2
Why This Is So Important To You Now............15

Why This Is So Important To You Now	16
Why This May Be For You	17
Why This May Not Be For You	18

Chapter 3
How We Got Here....................................21

How We Got Here	22
Our Big Epiphany	24
But There Was a Problem	25
And Then Things Changed	26
Then We Thought Massive and Things Turned Around	29
There's a Five-Step Strategy	31

Chapter 4
Choose Massive Growth............................33

Step One	34
1. Your Choice – Mediocre vs. Massive	35
Gerald's Story	37
Strategic Acquisition	39
Cross Marketing Multiplier	39
Efficiency Profits	42
No Promises	44

The Driving Force Massive
Business Growth Formula

Chapter 5
Find Your Massive Idea...................................47
Step Two	48
You'll Need Help From the Outside	48
One is the Most Dangerous Number in Business	49
Let's Get Started	52
Inner Circle Massive Idea Partners	53
Outer Circle Massive Idea Partners	54
Aircraft Carriers	57
The Conversation	61
6 Massive Growth Areas	64
To Start the Conversation	66
Idea Generator	69
Leadership	70
Management	71
Financials	72
Marketing	73
Sales	74
Production	75
Putting It All Together	76
This Works in Any Industry	77

Chapter 6
Massive Action Mode...............................…..83
Step Three	84
Empty Your Cup	84
Set Up a Massive Action Work Environment	85
Massive Action Work Environment Checklist	86
3-Golden Nuggets of Massive Action	87

Chapter 7
Connect Your Idea To Extraordinary People……….93
Step Four	94
How to Discover Who Your Extraordinary Connections Need to Be	96
Don't Be the Smartest Person in the Room	101
Do Individual Hotseats	102
Do Your Homework	103
Take a Day Off	104
Record Every Word of It	105
Pay For It	105
Get Uncomfortable	106

Chapter 8
Connect Your Idea To Extraordinary Resources...107
    Step Five   108
    The Resources You're Going To Need   108
    Negotiating to Get the Best Deal for Your Resources   111
    Know What Their Needs Are First   114
    Understand the Resource You Want Access to   115
    Understand Price Resources   118
    The Conversation Will Turn to Price   120
    Know Their Objections Before They Bring Them Up   122
    Take Ego Out of the Equation   127
    Don't Take Things Personally   128
    Be Wise About The Big Picture   129
    Look For Someone With Many More Resources   130
    The Resource Provider Should Do This Too   133
    Avoid the Use of "I"   133
    Good Table Manners Count   135
    Make This About the Issues   136
    Avoid Negotiating Piecemeal   137
    You Need to Do Your Homework   139
    You're Going to be Dealing With People You May Not Like   140
    Negotiate the Problems   141
    Make Sure They Have a Good Perception of You   142
    Communication, That's What It's All About   143
    Negotiations Within the Negotiations   144

Chapter 9
Your Next Step Is Easier Than You....................149
    Your Best Next Step Is Easier Than You Think   150
    The Right Questions   151
    Get Started Now   151
    Get a Guide   152
    This Is What You Need to do Now   152

Chapter 10
Worksheets..155

Notes...174

Introduction

Introduction

Welcome to The Driving Force Massive Business Growth Formula. This controversial book will expose you to a counterintuitive method that'll allow you to make massive, possibly exponential leaps of profitable growth in your business. This book will also erase the need for you to take years and years to grow your business to the level that you dreamed of the day you opened your doors for business or put your shingle out and started to accept customers, clients or patients for profit. It will forever end the need for you to follow the typical slow growth model that you see everyone else in your community, your region and even in your entire industry using. It will allow you to grow your business hundreds of times faster than 99.99% of the millions of US businesses while at the same time following the path that the fastest .01% of businesses are blazing. (Biery, "The State Of U.S. Small Businesses Entering 2016")

The Driving Force Massive Business Growth Formula was created by Walter Bergeron and Sam Frentzas, who have helped hundreds of clients to identify their biggest growth opportunities and dreams and then connect them with the resources they needed to make those dreams become a reality. This includes clients who have payed $100,000 or more for done for you marketing programs, and over $12,000 for a single day of consulting. They are the dynamic duo of facilitating business growth, being advised by business superstar Mr. Marcus Lemonis, famed star of CNBC's ® "The Profit®" and "The Partner®" as well as CEO of Camping World®, Good Sam® and many other companies. Their list of private clients is legendary, including Steve and Rick Cesari, the men responsible for the marketing genius behind George Foreman Grill®, Oxiclean®, Sonicare Toothbrush® and GoPro® Camera… to name a few.

Now, it's time for you to discover…

The Driving Force
Massive Business Growth Formula.

Chapter 1

The Unvarnished Truth

The Unvarnished Truth

I hope you're interested in the blunt, unvarnished truth about how entrepreneurs and small business owners really make massive leaps of growth in their businesses, create obscene amounts of profit and grow at a rate that on average is over 100 times faster than everyone else. Because quite frankly, not everyone is ready for such a conversation. Some prefer good excuses to stay where they are, small and underperforming, over not getting to this top level of business achievement. And yet still others actually prefer to live in a fantasy world rather than a world of cold, harsh reality.

I'm Walter Bergeron, here with my partner Sam Frentzas. What we're about to show you will radically alter how you plan and execute the future of your business. That's because you're about to become part of a movement called The Driving Force. It is impacting thousands of businesses, professions, industries, product and service categories, literally changing the way entrepreneurs view their industry, their business and their own personal financial future.

The Driving Force was created to help empower regular small business owners and entrepreneurs like you, with the ability to follow the path created by companies that blazed an already proven trail to massive business growth. It was created to show driven entrepreneurs how to aggressively and proactively plan and execute massive business growth by following the fastest growing and most successful companies in the U.S., rather than simply, blindly following everyone else in their industry as a lemming would over a cliff into a dark, deep chasm of mediocrity or worse yet, sitting back and waiting for growth to happen. Hope won't get you there, massive action will.

Entrepreneurs Need a Massive Growth Strategy

You need a faster, much more aggressive and proactive formula that focuses on growth in massive leaps, not the miniscule steps you see so often. You need a proven path to growth that significantly outpaces what others in your industry are doing, what your competitors are doing and what all other companies are doing. Small growth strategies mean slow growth strategies which adds frustration and most of the time the strategies are DEAD WRONG for your goals. Massive growth is the only way to make your business life significantly more pleasant, extremely lucrative, and absolutely certain to be successful.

You'll Need Help From the Outside

You need to know that you are not alone and should not attempt to go it alone. As we all know, one is the most limiting number in business. One idea can fail, one strategy can be wrong, one connection can be severed, one vendor can disappear, one key employee can go lame, one client can find another vendor, etc.

One is the Most Dangerous Number in Business

In other words, you'll need help. You'll need help in many ways and in order to get help you'll want to look externally so that not only do you not have to go it alone and do it alone but also so that you can expand your ideas beyond what you are capable of doing alone.

Idea Expansion to broaden your horizons is not a new concept but it is an essential strategy you'll need to embrace and fully adopt to maximize the power of getting help from others. So, looking at this another way, the only way to expand your ideas, to truly expand your thinking so that it doesn't snap back to its original size, like a rubber band, is to embrace the fact that you'll absolutely need to expand your entire network of external connections way beyond where it is currently.

This is called Idea Expansion. Idea Expansion, though a new term to you, is already a natural part of the business community. It exists everywhere and has existed since the cavemen began accepting payment of round stones in exchange for the miracle of fire. You probably do it without even knowing it. Likely you've got a few other business Idea Expansion books on your bookshelf besides this one. So, getting points of view from the outside is already a part of how you operate, that's a small sample of Idea Expansion. Now let's make it an even bigger part of your strategy to massively grow your business and realize your dreams.

Idea Expansion also comes from the company you keep, the people you surround yourself with and even the mentors you engage with. Napolean Hill, the author of "Think and Grow Rich" had Andrew Carnegie the great steel tycoon. Even Andrew Carnegie had Thomas Scott the railroad tycoon as both a mentor and advisor. In more recent times, Mark Zuckerberg of Facebook had Steve Jobs, Bill Gates of Microsoft had Warren Buffett, and Richard Branson had Sir Freddy Laker, another British Airline tycoon.

So, by surrounding yourself with people who are better, smarter, faster, richer than you are not only expands your ideas but also connects you to the multiplicative effect of the mastermind. It is also worth realizing that these alliances happen, not by chance by the way, outside each other's industries. A steel tycoon helps an author, a railroad tycoon helps a steel industry expert, hardware helping software, different industries taking advice, mentorship and ideas from the outside and bringing them in as new fresh strategies. Well-worn strategies and tactics that seem stale and obsolete in one industry become fresh and new and revolutionary when brought into another industry. This concept is not new, but it is very important and can be very powerful when embraced and used to its fullest potential.

Now you may not believe in the metaphysical or even paranormal side of the mastermind effect or its' ability to multiply a magnetic force that actually draws form a larger Universal Intelligence as Napolean Hill did. But you must at the very least embrace the power of the mastermind effect for its multiplying effect through the merging of minds. It is interesting to note that rarely are any companies ever built without the power of having this type of partnership or at the very least a small number of connections they use in conjunction with the mastermind concept. So go forward knowing that you are on the right path as you follow in the footsteps of giants who have blazed this trail for you.

Connections to Extraordinary People

Idea implementation is also about the execution of that idea in addition to the quality of the idea and to do that with maximum effectiveness you'll need connections to extraordinary people. Those connections will give you three distinct advantages. First, unfettered access to private information, secondly, use of diverse skills, and lastly a unique power of additional connections.

You'll need to take a proactive approach to make these connections deep and meaningful connections on multiple levels in order for this to have any real meaning for your business growth. Just as Hill had Carnegie and Gates had Buffett you too will need connections that are beyond your initial grasp and level of influence. You'll need a system and help to get these valuable connections.

Private Information

In these days access to more information, more public information, is not an asset, it is not a strategic advantage and it is not helpful for massive business growth. Quite the opposite actually. It is overwhelming, distracting and a true time-suck on an already limited and valuable resource, your time. What you need is private information, private knowledge and private experiences that are wholly focused on your business and even more focused on massive business growth ideas and implementation to give you an edge. In a trusted network of connections this knowledge and this edge you gain can turn your big idea into massive growth. Be it a new product or service being released that you can take advantage of, or what a particular large client needs or is looking for a solution for, or even how to gain access to even more important connections so you can expand your network.

In our own experience in our attempt to connect with Marcus Lemonis we had to go through three tiers of people to get a personal audience with him, three levels of connections that took us months to build and foster. There was a constant give and take to truly connect to these people on multiple levels before we could get the access we truly desired to help us grow our connection and then in turn, grow our business.

Diverse Skills

Then and only then did we have access to another important part of these extraordinary personal connections and that was to connect to diverse and possibly even unique skill set. One of our clients, Steve and Rick Cesari are such examples.

Steve and Rick are the marketing geniuses behind the creation of some of the most recognizable and powerful household brands. You may have heard of George Foreman Grill, Sonicare Toothbrush, Oxiclean and GoPro camera. To make these names as big as they are required a skill set, dare I say even a unique skill set when you consider the environment that Steve and Rick encountered as they helped build these companies and brands. And only through powerful and extraordinary personal connections can you get access to such a skill set and then use that skill set to your advantage.

Power of Additional Connections

Then, last, but certainly not the least of your reasons to connect to extraordinary people, is the power of additional connections they bring to the table. You may not always have or even need connections that are at the top of the ladder to get the greatest impact, but all of the people you are connected to will also have other people they are connected to that can be of great advantage to you. The power to expand your network is directly proportional to the number of connections that your connections have.

So, once you identify your massive business growth idea and connect that idea to your extraordinary network, they will help you find the massive ways to implement your idea to save you time, money and just as importantly help you to avoid stepping into the inevitable pothole on your journey toward massive growth.

Connections to Extraordinary Resources

The idea of connecting to extraordinary resources is the strategic use of the resources of other companies as well as other people's resources so that you can save time to accomplish your goals. It is one of the quickest and easiest ways to fast-track the development of a massive business idea so that your business can hit the big time quickly, there is no advantage of slow growth and profit. Time being the key factor in all of this.

Extraordinary resources are particularly useful in the start-up phase of a new business idea, since it is very likely that you won't likely have all of the capital to pay full retail for everything that you'll need to get done to fully implement your idea at the level you want it to launch at.

But there is also another side to this that you must avoid. Since entrepreneurs are often victims of their 'can-do' attitude you must be smarter than your failures and creatively use the extraordinary resources of others to accomplish all you have set to accomplish. Remember that by simply doing more of what you do, you are simply leveraging your resources, essentially achieving more through the efficient use of your own resources. Leverage can be using you or your employees time, talents, skills, contacts, credibility and resources. This is a way to help to take more advantage of our most limiting resource which is time. But there is a much better way to use leverage than simply leveraging your resources.

Since we only have a limited number of hours per day to accomplish all we need to accomplish and by working on the massive growth idea all by our lonesome you are actually putting a huge roadblock in your own way. But by also connecting to other people's extraordinary resources, you will acquire a true asset for your business expansion. Though it does require a departure from conventional thinking about how to get things done, you are essentially eliminating the bottleneck to your production by having many, many bottles to develop your idea through and therefore fast track your success. So, by all means use your time more efficiently and leverage all of your own assets to maximize the deployment of your idea, but also use the assets of others to exponentially grow your idea.

How to Read This Book

So, if you ever want to massively grow your business in this current business environment then we urge you, for the sake of your family, to keep reading. We are going to show you a proven path to exponential growth and how to achieve financial freedom and time freedom so that you can live the lifestyle you always dreamed that your business could provide to you and your family.

You've taken the first steps toward learning a life-changing model for massive growth for your business. This book is your road map, along the way we'll show you what you need to do and when you need to do it. Along the way there'll be brainstorming sessions, worksheets and lots of planning and implementation. Mark the pages, crease the corners, highlight the pages and passages most relevant to your business and use this book as an invaluable weapon in your business arsenal. It's crucial to know each chapter in detail but more importantly you need to know how to gather a team behind you to support you in your efforts as well as help you when you need deeper, more penetrating knowledge and experience as you massively grow your business.

Chapter 2

Why This Is So Important To

Why This is Important to You Now

Now you're probably asking yourself "Why is this important to me?" And more specifically, "Why is it important to me right now?"

The answer - TIME

Time is not on your side, it's not on my side, it's not on the side of any entrepreneur with dreams of having their business, their enterprise become something of significance and impact in their lives. Time is not on your side if you have unrealized dreams for your business, things you want to do with your business, places you want to take your business and rewards you want to reap by accomplishing these things. So, your enemy is time.

If you've ever attempted to aggressively grow your business, you have probably realized that most growth strategies are frustratingly slow. They focus on miniscule growth ideas that result in miniscule growth or no growth at all, taking more and more time until your goals are reached. Or they make promises of growth that there's no way you'll be able to achieve unless you have all the advantages of the person telling you or of a specific industry trend. Wasting even more time on bad ideas and false starts.

We're going to show you exactly how you can stop wasting your time on business growth strategies that don't work or grow you in an excruciatingly slow manner, something that's so frustrating. and that you don't have to be like the 99.99% companies only growing at a miniscule average of only 7.8%. (Biery, "The State Of U.S. Small Businesses Entering 2016") You can proactively and aggressively be like the .01% that grows at an astonishing average of 1,772%. (Buchanan, "What the Companies on the Inc. 5000 All Have in Common")

Why This May Be For You

This book is for you if you're frustrated because your business growth has become stagnant. This book is for you if you're frustrated by slow organic business growth and there don't seem to be any options on changing that. This book is for you if you're tired of spending money on programs and consultants, and coaches and trainings, without getting the big results that they're promising. This book is for you if you're overwhelmed with all the many, thousands of choices of business growth being pushed at you from every direction but no proof that any of it actually works. This book is really and truly for you if you feel like no one understands what you're trying to accomplish with your business. This book is for you if all other solutions that you're being offered seem small, seem insignificant, seem like growing but in only a very small way. This book is for you if you've given up on your big dreams of massive growth or if you've given up on doing something really spectacular with your business, and no one seems to be able to get you where you want to go. This book is for you.

Why This May NOT Be For You

This book in NOT for you if you're looking for a "get rich quick" scheme, because this process and strategy docs take time to do it right. This book in NOT for you if you want to do nothing and get paid, because this does take significant work to accomplish, as does anything worth doing. There is a lot of work involved, and the results that I'm going to show you aren't typical. I won't make any promises that you can do this at all. Most people who buy or use or get any kind of online how to make money training will never make a nickel whatsoever. It's just like the piece of exercise equipment you have sitting in the corner of your room, it won't give you any results if you don't actually use it. I won't make any promises here whatsoever and you should be skeptical of anyone that does make bold promises.

Chapter 3

How We Got Here

How We Got Here

Before we move on, I want to tell you exactly how we got here, just in case you're wondering why in the world you're listening to both of us here. Sam and I started a company called Red Carpet Business Marketing, we're doing done-for-you direct marketing services. We have a real skill for it, all of the last businesses we've both owned used this kind of direct marketing system to grow them organically and we wanted to provide these services to other entrepreneurs that needed these services to grow their own businesses.

Now we knew we had to start with the foundational growth strategies, just like every business does. Standard and foundational direct marketing principles, one-on-one sales, trade shows, social media, newsletters, direct mail, email, internal sales staff, joint ventures and events. We used these typical, cautious and small scale growth strategies, just like everyone else does in our industry, and like everyone else advised. The reason we followed what was advised to us is because that's the only way that they knew how to grow this business. Now at first the business started growing at a rate we were proud of and well above that national average of 7.8%. (Biery, "The State Of U.S. Small Businesses Entering 2016") We got off the ground very quickly, acquired a few clients, saw significant profit levels and things were going very well. But then, as the business started to mature, the growth started to level off, to flat-line and we weren't growing nearly as fast that we wanted to, what we envisioned was possible for our business. At this rate we were never going to reach the goals we set for our business, we were never going to make the big impact in our industry and we were sure as hell never going to reap the huge rewards we were driven to receive as a result of getting to these goals.

So, like you might do, just as we had done with our previous businesses, and just like everyone else would do; we repeated and modeled what everyone else in our industry was doing to grow. We copied the strategies of the mediocre and hoped that by doing a better job at what they were doing, that this would solve our problems of growth and help us accomplish the dreams we had for our business. Stupid, right? How could that possibly work? We actually started doing more of the same old thing everyone else was doing and actually wondered why in the hell it wasn't working. We wondered why we were so damn frustrated. Looking back now I guess that's kind of silly, because why would we get different results if we continued to do the same old thing over and over and over again? Why would we actually get results that were different from what everyone else was getting when we were doing the exact same thing they were doing. Needless to say, that plan wasn't getting us where we wanted to go.

So just how do you get out of that kind of a rut? How do you make absolutely certain you stop going down that path and change directions right away? Well, our first step was to identify what everyone else was doing and everything we were doing that they were doing and we made a big ol' list. Then we stopped doing every single one of those things. We knew that, those things weren't getting us where we wanted to go and they flat out weren't working. Those ideas and strategies were only getting us at the single-digit growth, just like everyone else.

Our Big Epiphany

Our big idea was to do something different, our epiphany was to go against the current, go against the grain and do the exact opposite of what everyone else was doing.

Instead of looking internally to our own industry for the answers, modeling those who have had some small level of success, we wanted much, much, much larger success. So, we sought out those who had succeeded on a grand scale. We looked for those people that had grown their business at lightning speed, that it got into a much, much larger level than we can ever do, someone who had gotten to the billion-dollar level, the 10-figure level. Because we knew that if we could only achieve a tiny bit of their success, just replicate a smidgen of their fortune by following the model that those billionaire businesses used to grow their business, that would still result in huge growth for our business.

But There Was a Problem

We didn't know any billionaires. We had no idea on who the hell we're going to talk to, who we were going to strive to model their process. I didn't know any billionaires that were going to talk to me one-on-one, look at our little marketing business, and tell us what we had to do to grow in massive ways. I know my partner Sam didn't know any of their either. We had no idea who the hell we were going to talk to. We had quite a dilemma and were once again frustrated as hell because no one could give us the answers that we needed to grow our business like we wanted to.

We had had some success, but the success wasn't continuing, it was just the slow, mediocre growth, and no one had any brand-new ideas to grow us in this really big way. We felt like our dreams were going to be dashed because we didn't know the right people. We sure as hell didn't have the right resources to get us there, and we were going to wind up doing the same old damn thing, just like everyone else in our industry was doing. There we were at a dead end, completely yet frustrated again.

And Then Things Changed

Now I remember when this major breakthrough happened. It was actually on a Wednesday morning. The only reason I remember it was a Wednesday morning is because the CNBC show "The Profit" with Marcus Lemonis comes on, on Tuesday nights. Sam and I spoke the next morning and we had both watched the show the night before. And that's when the change happened, BAM! It was right then that we both said, "Holy crap, here is a billionaire and he's actually showing us on television how he's growing these businesses, and he has a billion-dollar business."

Now look, I know it's reality TV, it's reality real, not real-real, the business growth is hyped and the drama is enhanced for TV, and we took that with a grain of salt. We realized that, "Of course, not everything as it appears to be," but Marcus really was the CEO of a company doing multiple billions of dollars, with many, many locations. He really and truly was investing in these companies with his own money. We figured that he would be a guy that could do this for us or at least definitely one of the top three guys that could help us.

We also realized that he was a pretty down-to-earth guy. Everything he was showing on the show wasn't all silver linings, there were a lot of pitfalls, a lot of failures. He was showing us what goes wrong, as well as what goes right. We decided that it would be in our best interest to try to contact Marcus or at least figure out exactly how he could advise us on growing our business.

Now, why Marcus? I mean, he wasn't in our industry. To our knowledge he had no idea how to grow a marketing business, but we thought that was a real plus for us because he could give us a different perspective on how to grow our business. The real question is, "Would he?" I don't know that we could offer Marcus anything that would get him to take us on as a pet project, to do a one-on-one call with us, to give us some one-on-one advice. We had no idea how to get in touch with him.

So, we started at square one. We tried to get in touch with his agent. Now we had no idea who this was. We had to do quite a bit of research to figure out who his real agent was. Then we had to go through a quite extensive application process just to get a conversation with his agent. There were down payments and a lot of hoops to jump through to even get a call with his agent.

Now I wish I could tell you that what happened was Marcus heard about our story, and he agreed to put us on the show and things went all perfect for us, but that's not what happened at all. As a matter of fact, quite the opposite happened. We had our first call with his agent, and we blew it. We totally blew it. We were completely unprepared. We didn't know the right questions to ask. We didn't know the right answers to give him. We had nothing to offer Marcus, because the questions that his agent asked us had nothing to do with us simply paying Marcus, because it's not about money in order to have a conversation with Marcus Lemonis. As a matter of fact, that never even came up. We had to offer Marcus something spectacularly good enough on top of paying him, in order for him to even have a conversation with his agent. We blew it the first time. We had all the wrong answers, didn't have the money that we needed to pay him, and he wasn't interested in doing any kind of one-on-one consulting with us.

Then We Thought Massive and Things Turned Around

But as hardheaded and driven entrepreneurs, we didn't take no for an answer. We had to figure out a way to get Marcus to do this, and we had to think differently in order to get a different result. So we thought about a solution that would get us the desired result, a process that we'll walk you through in the rest of this book. A process to get you to find your massive growth idea step by step so you can have the same type of results that we achieved.

Oh, just in case you're wondering if this worked for us you can take a look at this link here. www.TheDrivingForceBook.com You can see Marcus Lemonis actually at our event, speaking about the very same product here. The very same program here that we'd love you to get involved in, this is our Mastermind Group. Marcus is actually speaking about our Mastermind Group. With this big idea, with this massive growth idea, with all the connections we had, with a lot of perseverance, with using all the resources we can get a hold of, and thinking outside of just mediocre growth, thinking about massive growth, we actually were able to achieve the goal that we wanted. We are achieving the growth level we wanted, look out for us on that Inc. 500 list because here we come very quickly, because of this growth that we're experiencing, and it's because we had a huge idea.

Now as we got past this, we looked back and realized that we were right on target, just like the other 20 million businesses in the US. I don't know if you know this or not, but according to Forbes Magazine, of the roughly

5.5 million US businesses that actually have employees, 99.99% of those businesses that have less than $5 million in annual revenue only have a 7.5% average annual sales growth. (Biery, "The State Of U.S. Small Businesses Entering 2016") But while these $5.5 million businesses are only growing at 7.8%, the top Inc. 5000 businesses are growing at an average of 1,772%. (Buchanan, "What the Companies on the Inc. 5000 All Have in Common")

1,772% is huge compared to 7.8% and the reason there is such a dramatic difference is because those businesses chose a path of massive growth instead of mediocre growth that everyone else accepts. So just as we did in deciding that mediocre growth was not for us, you too can decide to stop settling for what everyone else is getting and reach the top 5000 business who are driven to reach the 1,772% growth and we have the process here for you to do just that. (Buchanan, "What the Companies on the Inc. 5000 All Have in Common")

There's a Five-Step Strategy

The five-step strategy that those achieving massive growth are using, a strategy that we used, to make massive leaps of growth in their business is this. First and foremost you must choose massive growth and then secondly find your massive growth idea. Then you'll need to get into massive action mode so that you can connect that idea to extraordinary people and extraordinary resources. That's what we're going to go over next, how you can do this for yourself.

Chapter 4

Choose Massive Growth

Step One

Step one is to choose that you truly want massive growth in your business. In order to achieve this massive growth you simply need to choose that you want massive growth versus mediocre growth. Decide that you are unwilling to continue to settle for the same old way everyone else is growing. You won't settle for the ancestral way others in your industry are growing. You want massive growth. I know it seems really simple, it seems like, "Well, duh, I wouldn't be here, reading this book if I didn't want to grow massively," but it's one thing to say that in your head, it's another thing to write it down and to actually put this down on paper, so that you do take action on that massive growth.

What I want you to do right now, is I would like you to think about what is the amount of growth that your business has had over the last three years, and write that number down. If it's negative growth, put negative whatever the percentage is. If you don't know it, if you have to go back to your profit loss statement, then I want you to make an educated guess. Give a good rough estimate on what your annual growth rate has been over the last three years on your profit loss statement. If it's 5%, write that down below on this worksheet, 10%, 50%, whatever the amount is write that down on your worksheet, so at least you know where you're starting. I want you to know that it's important to know where you're starting, because I want you to see that maybe that this mediocre growth will show you why you're frustrated with your current growth rate in your business. It's because the growth rate isn't where you want it to be, and that's actually step two.

1. Your Choice – Mediocre vs. Massive

What is your average year to year growth?

_____

The next thing I want you to do is to write down the number that you'd like your business to grow at. Would you like it to grow at a 1,000%? That would be your business growing at 10 times its size right now or maybe you want it to grow at 17 or 20 times the size it is right now, that's the rate at which the Inc. 500's are growing. Some of these guys on the Inc. 500 list are growing at

30,000%, that's 300 times their current size. That is huge amount of growth.

What do you ideally want your growth to be next year?

_____

What I want you to do right now is to write down where you are, and I want you to write down where you want to go. Is it 10 times your current size? Then write down 1,000% on the sheet of paper. I know you think it's insignificant, but write it down. Make sure you don't move forward until you physically write these numbers down. Don't just think them in your head, put them down on paper. You will not tolerate the 7.8% growth rate that 99.99% of businesses are doing. I want you to know that you will not settle for that mediocre growth, you want massive growth.

Now, when we were stuck in that growth rate in our marketing business we put down a growth rate of 1,000%. When we decided we wanted to grow it by 10 times, and we're on track to do that, and it was because we were able to get our big idea to come to fruition. Choosing massive growth is the best first step and it can look a lot of different ways.

Here's another way to do it, a client of ours in the pest control industry achieved massive growth with another type of massive idea. Here's his story.

Gerald's Story

Gerald owns a pest control company, he's an exterminator by trade, meaning he goes into peoples' houses and gets rid of their bugs and unwanted pests. He is a humble, but driven, blue-collar entrepreneur and I consider it my calling to guide him to his financial liberation. So, Gerald's pest control company was grossing around $600k in annual revenue and around 10% profit. A comfortable living for him and his wife and children but nowhere near large enough to reach his growth goal, he calls it his enough is enough number.

Gerald's massive growth idea is a process called growth stacking, and it works like this. Gerald would seek out and strategically buy other companies and merge them with his company. Then he would use 3 growth models and exponentially grow his company and then sell the much larger, much more profitable company after he reached his growth goal and someone offered him his enough is enough number for the business. For Gerald, that process looked like this:

He searched for a company that:

1. Had around the same gross revenue as his company, so he could afford to do this deal comfortably.

Actually, the way this deal was structured Gerald walked away from the closing with many thousands of dollars in his pocket, through a process called a full leveraged buyout.

2. Had the same type of clients but no overlap between his current clients and the acquisition company clients

3. He made sure there was lots of duplication of company business processes.

And I'll get into why he wanted that in a second.

Once he found a company that met these three goals he made the purchase.

Gerald made a…

Strategic Acquisition

At closing his <u>$600k business became a $1.2 million company</u>, not a bad day to be able to double the size of your company at the stroke of a pen.

But this is just the tip of the iceberg when it comes to massive growth through Growth-Stacking.

Step two of Growth-Stacking is called the…

Cross Marketing Multiplier

Do you remember when I told you that Gerald bought a company that met his goals? You might have noticed that none of his goals for his Strategic Acquisition of the right company had anything to do with the type of services they offered, just that they had identical client types.

Gerald actually bought an air conditioning company, an HVAC company, these are the guys that come to your house and repair your heating or air-conditioning system. Now Gerald certainly could have bought another pest control company, to most entrepreneurs this would be the most logical choice, stick with what you know.

But Gerald was thinking strategically and used Growth Stacking to maximize the amount of his growth.

He knew that by acquiring another company and focusing on the clients, that the services weren't a critical criteria for the purchase. As a matter of a fact, had Gerald bought another pest control company <u>he would not have been able to take advantage of the Cross Marketing Multiplier.</u>

The Cross Marketing Multiplier works like this.

Gerald took his pest control services and offered those services to his newly acquired clients and in a very short time, since he already had a great relationship with his clients from the purchase of the new business, he quickly increased his revenue by another multiple. Gerald marketed his pest control service to the air conditioning clients and went from $1.2 million to $1.8 million.

But Gerald certainly didn't stop there.

He then took his newly acquired air conditioning services and offered those services to his pest control clients. And since he had a great relationship with those clients as well *Gerald's company went from $1.8 million to $2.4 million.* This is something absolutely possible when using massive growth through Strategic Acquisition. **There is no faster or easier way to double the size of your client list** AND have that very critical already established bond, that well developed relationship with your clients, all with the stroke of a pen. And it is because of this previously established relationship that the Cross Marketing Multiplier works. But Gerald didn't stop there either. Remember that one of Gerald's criteria for the company he was going to buy was that they had a duplication of business processes, meaning that both companies had a human resources department and accounting and sales and marketing departments and personnel and equipment. Well, as a savvy entrepreneur, Gerald implemented step three of growth-stacking called...

Efficiency Profits

Efficiency profits increases growth by another multiple by eliminating all of the duplication between the two companies. By eliminating duplicate expenses in personnel, real estate, business equipment, this change increases profits substantially. Then on top of the elimination of expenses you add back in efficiency by keeping the best of the best parts of both business processes. These two factors enabled Gerald to add another multiple of value to the company while at the same time increasing profits by another 10%.

Summary

Part one, (see figure 1) Gerald did one *Strategic Acquisition* and on day one at the closing he doubled the size of his company from *$600k to $1.2* million and walked out of the deal with no up-front costs and with a few thousand dollars in his pocket by doing a fully leveraged buyout.

Part two, (see figure 1) Gerald implemented the ***Cross Marketing Multiplier*** and within a few months he had cross-marketed the services of both companies, since he now had a list of clients that doubled in size at the closing.

So, he went from ***$1.2 million to $1.8*** million by selling air conditioning services to pest control clients and then went from ***$1.8 million to $2.4*** million by offering his pest control services to his air conditioning clients.

Then part three, (see figure 1) he implemented ***Efficiency Profits*** and eliminated duplicate expenses and increased the efficiency of both companies and went from ***$2.4 million to $3 million dollars***. So, with Growth Stacking his business size increased by 5 times and his profits went from 10% of $600k, so $60k to 20% of $3 million, that's $600k.

That's 1000% business growth

That's the power of a properly executed, well-engineered massive growth strategy.

And now since Gerald was more experienced in the Growth Stacking process he did this once more and this time shot the size of his business up to over *$12 million.*

No Promises Here

Now I want to emphasize that **I cannot promise or guarantee that you can do this**, you need to make this decision and decide if this is right for you. But, I would urge you to do a little homework and look at how fast growing companies are making huge moves. Look at what venture capitalists are doing, and look at what the large players in your market are doing to achieve massive growth and market share. I think you will find that strategic acquisitions play a large role and that it would be a great opportunity for you to exponentially grow your business.

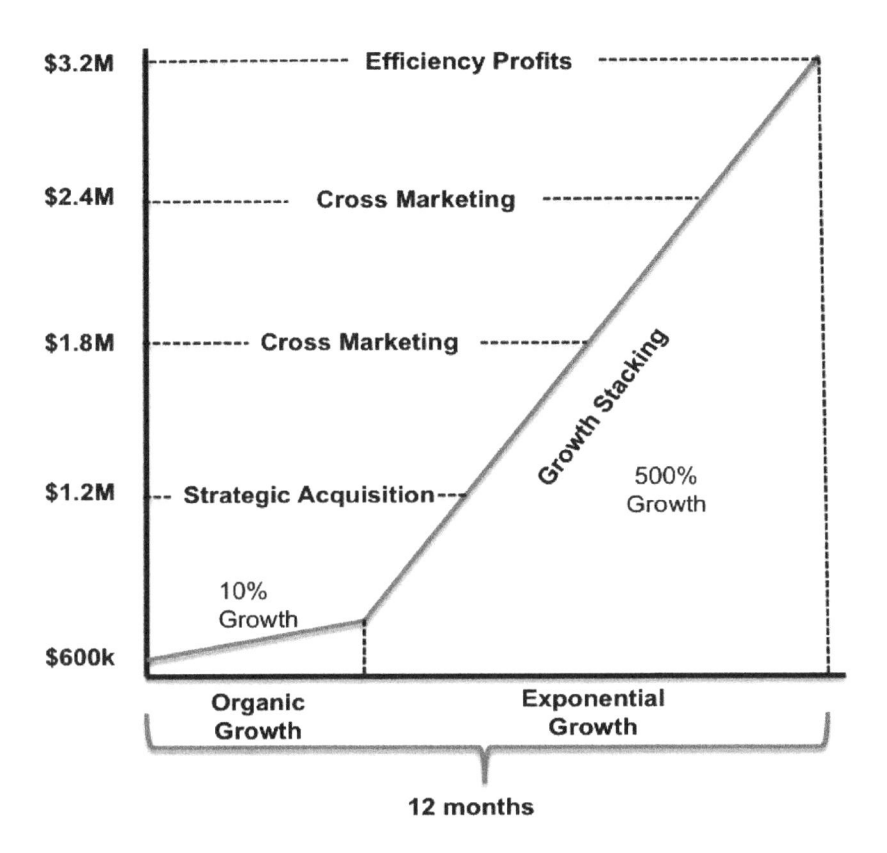

You're Only One Idea Away From Massive Business Growth
Go to www.TheDrivingForceBook.com to get Your FREE Gift Worth $747.83

(Figure 1)

Chapter 4/Choose Massive Growth 45

Chapter 5

Find Your Massive Idea

Step Two

How do you go about finding these Massive Growth Ideas? Where do they appear? When Sam and I had got our first Massive Growth Idea, it didn't just appear on our horizon, we actually thought about it together. Now, not only did we think about that idea, I didn't tell you the exact whole story, but we had the idea the next morning about what Marcus might be able to give us, but we actually had more than one person on that list. As a matter of fact, it took a few weeks for us to come up with this big idea on exactly how to get Marcus, and how to get him to come to our event. It took outside our industry thinking, it took an outside perspective, outside of just us as business partners, and our inner circle of people we knew. We reached far outside to find our Massive Growth Idea.

You'll Need Help From the Outside

As you read before, you need to know that you are not alone and should not attempt to go it alone. As we all know, one is the most limiting number in business. One idea can fail, one strategy can be wrong, one connection can be severed, one vendor can disappear, one key employee can go lame, one client can find another vendor, etc.

One is the Most Dangerous Number in Business.

In other words, you'll need help. You'll need help in many ways and in order to get help you'll want to look externally so that not only do you not have to go it alone and do it alone but also so that you can expand your ideas beyond what you are capable of doing alone.

Idea expansion to broaden your horizons is not a new concept but it is an essential strategy you'll need to embrace and fully adopt to maximize the power of getting help from others. So, looking at this another way, the only way to expand your ideas, to truly expand your thinking so that it doesn't snap back to its original size, like a rubber band, is to embrace the fact that you'll absolutely need to expand your entire network of external connections way beyond where it is currently.

This is called Idea Expansion. Idea Expansion, though a new term to you, is already a natural part of the business community. It exists everywhere and has existed since the cavemen began accepting payment of round stones in exchange for the miracle of fire. You probably do it without even knowing it. Likely you've got a few other business Idea Expansion books on your bookshelf besides this one. So, getting points of view from the outside is already a part of how you operate, that's a small sample of Idea Expansion. Now let's make it an even bigger part of your strategy to massively grow your business and realize your dreams.

Idea Expansion also comes from the company you keep, the people you surround yourself with and even the mentors you engage with. Napolean Hill, the author of "Think and Grow Rich" had Andrew Carnegie the great steel tycoon. Even Andrew Carnegie had Thomas Scott the railroad tycoon as both a mentor and advisor. In more recent times, Mark Zuckerberg of Facebook had Steve Jobs, Bill Gates of Microsoft had Warren Buffett, and Richard Branson had Sir Freddy Laker, another British Airline tycoon.

So, by surrounding yourself with people who are better, smarter, faster, richer than you are not only expands your ideas but also connects you to the multiplicative effect of the mastermind. It is also worth realizing that these alliances happen, not by chance by the way, outside each other's industries. A steel tycoon helps an author, a railroad tycoon helps a steel industry expert, hardware helping software, different industries taking advice, mentorship and ideas from the outside and bringing them in as new fresh strategies. Well-worn strategies and tactics that seem stale and obsolete in one industry become fresh and new and revolutionary when brought into another industry. This concept is not new, but it is very and can be very powerful when embraced and used to its fullest potential.

Now you may not believe in the metaphysical or even paranormal side of the mastermind effect or its' ability to multiply a magnetic force that actually draws form a larger Universal Intelligence as Napolean Hill did. But you must at the very least embrace the power of the mastermind effect for its multiplying effect through the merging of minds. It is interesting to note that rarely are any companies ever built without the power of having this type of partnership or at the very least a small number of connections they use in conjunction with the mastermind concept. So, go forward knowing that you are on the right path as you follow in the footsteps of giants who have blazed this trail for you.

Let's Get Started!

What I want you to know first, is that you don't have the corner on the market on new, fresh business growth ideas. Whether it's just you running your business or you and a partner or even you and a board of directors, whatever it is, don't just look internally for these business growth ideas. Looking externally is extremely powerful, and it's the way you're going to be able to expand beyond your own horizons. I want to show you how to step into a focused zone, where you're not necessarily comfortable with these ideas, but this zone will spark some new fresh ideas allowing new fresh brainstorming to come in, and actually give you potentially the big idea you're looking for.

I am going to walk you through this process of identifying your Massive Idea Partners, so get out your worksheet out and ready. Your massive idea partners are going to be someone that you're going to use to have some very specific guided conversations with about 6 areas of your business. I want to break down your Massive Idea Partners into 2 groups, your Inner Circle and Outer Circle. Your Inner Circle is anyone who has intimate knowledge of the workings of your business that you most likely look to regularly for business guidance. Your Outer Circle is anyone that doesn't have intimate knowledge of the inner workings of your business, but you think might be able to offer a different perspective on how to grow your business. I'll explain in a second on exactly what you want to do during the conversation, but first I want you to do is to identify and write down who is part of your Inner Circle and Outer Circle. I have given you some examples of each Circle below

Inner Circle Massive Idea Partners

Anyone inside the 4 walls of your business or with an intimate knowledge of the workings of your business that you most likely look to regularly for business guidance. These partners will have a certain perspective of your business, but also will have experiences outside of your business that may lead to massive idea. Remember, most likely they all have had jobs at other businesses and could have valuable ideas and insights that will help your business. Here are some ideas for your inner circle list.

1. **Spouse**
2. **Board of Directors**
3. **Vice President**
4. **Family**
5. **Employees**
6. **Investors**
7. **Partners**

First, brainstorm and put down anyone that comes to mind. Then I want you to go back and mark your top 5 and put them on your worksheet.

Outer Circle Massive Idea Partners

These will be individuals that don't have intimate knowledge of the inner workings of your business, but you think might be able to offer a different perspective on how to grow your business. Ideally these people are other business owners or people who run entire divisions of a business, that can give you some ideas on how they're experiencing success within their industry and with their business. They may be people that you know that are probably within your industry or at least you're connected with them in some way. Maybe they're your consultants, maybe they're your coaches, maybe they're people you're in a mastermind with already. Maybe they're people that you go to lunch with or watch a football game with, that just happens to also own businesses. Those are people that I want you to connect with, that's your outer circle list. Here are some ideas for you.

1. Business Owners – Competitors
2. Business Owners – Outside Your Industry
3. Coaches/Consultants/Masterminds
4. Your Vendors
5. Your CPA
6. Your Lawyer
7. Your Banker
8. Management Consultant

Again, brainstorm and put down anyone that comes to mind. Then I want you to go back and mark your top 5 and put them on your worksheet.

The top five Inner Circle people and the top five Outer Circle people, that would give you a good list of at least 10 people that you can connect with to help you get to your massive ideas and those would be your top 10 massive idea partners.

Worksheet - Top 10 Massive Idea Partners

Inner Circle   Outer Circle

1._____   1._____
2._____   2._____
3._____   3._____
4._____   4._____
5._____   5._____

A Quick Little Story from Walter Bergeron About Aircraft Carriers

A really quick story. As I mentioned earlier, I was a US Navy sailor. I spent six years in the US Navy, a couple years of nuclear engineering training and another four years aboard an aircraft carrier named the USS Carl Vinson, CVN 70. It was a nuclear-powered aircraft carrier that was part of what's called The Seventh Fleet. We were stationed on the West Coast in Bremerton, Washington, then down to Alameda, California, and then finally down to San Diego. Anyway, I was a part of the nuclear propulsion plant team that ran the two nuclear power plants. There's two big nuclear power plants aboard the carrier. I was one of the reactor operators on one of those plants.

As most anyone who's ever seen anything about the U.S. Navy, the aircraft carrier is a significant part of this fleet.

It's a significant part of the U.S. military arsenal. It's a huge vessel. It's almost 1,100 feet long. It's 100,000 tons of fighting machine. It's got two big old power plants.

We got our own mail system. It's, of course, an airport there with an aircraft storage area. It's got nuclear reactors, which is a huge part of the ship. We got our own laundry.

Essentially, it's a floating city. There's 5,500 people aboard that ship. It's significant. It's the biggest ship, by far, of any within the fleet. Honestly, when most people think about the U.S. Navy, for the most part, they think about aircraft carriers.

It's the show of power whenever this fleet of vessels goes anywhere. It is what everyone focuses on and sees as the true value of the military.

The reality is, is that if we had only aircraft carriers, if that's the only ship that the U.S. Navy ever built, it would fail in a heartbeat because the carrier's just one small portion of it. As a matter of fact, the carrier, while it looks like it is extremely powerful, that it projects this huge power to anyone that sees it, is actually very vulnerable. If you've ever seen the carrier, very rarely will you ever notice that it's alone.

There's a reason for that. It's because it is very vulnerable to attack from all sorts of ways. What you may not see below the surface is that there are a number of submarines that are always defending the carrier because it's very weak from the bottom. We actually had torpedoes onboard the carrier to help us fight if we ever came into battle where the submarines were not able to help us, but there's no way that we could actually fight off a submarine attack because we just weren't prepared to handle it. Bottom line, we were air superiority, while in the water we were super vulnerable.

While the carrier looks like it is the most important part of the fleet, the other 20 or 30, depending on what size of fleet we're going to have or what formation, the other vessels are extremely important. The carrier could not function without all this other defense, all this other support activity. That's really just like a business.

Most business owners just look at their marketing and sales to grow their business. But, like the carrier, remember the carrier is big & sexy, sales and marketing are too. They're big! Huge! It's what everyone sees and tries to replicate.

As a driven entrepreneur looking for massive growth, looking at just the sales area is a terrible way to grow, it's like handcuffing yourself to something. When looking at the carrier of a fleet, while it's impressive, it's not the only value, just like the sales and marketing areas of your business are not the only growth areas of your company. Just like the Naval Fleet, you have several areas of your business that support your marketing and sales efforts. You also have leadership, management, financial, and production. Now, it doesn't really matter if you don't have all six of these named divisions in your business, but for your business to run, you have all these are six areas working together to keep your business running effectively. And each of these could have a Massive Growth Idea hidden in them! It is important to look at all 6 Massive Growth Areas in your business, and not just sales and marketing, like most typical businesses are doing. Looking at just these 2 areas will ensure that you will continue with your mediocre growth, and never truly experience massive growth.

The Conversation

So now we have identified your top 10 Massive Idea Partners and your 6 Massive Growth Areas. What do you do with all of this? Now you need a proven plan to have organized and orchestrated conversations with your Massive Idea Partners, making sure that you look in detail at all six of these Massive Growth Areas in your business, Leadership, Management, Finances, Marketing, Sales and Production. You will want to ask some leading questions to guide the conversation in the most focused direction so that you can get the most from valuable time with your Massive Idea Partner and identify your Massive Growth Idea quickly. Your Massive Idea could be hidden in any of these 6 Massive Growth Areas.

The way we flush out these massive ideas in your business is that we will compare what you are doing in your business in the 6 Massive Growth Areas with what your Massive Idea Partner is doing in his business in these 6 areas. If you are both doing the same thing and have similar ideas then maybe there is no room for an idea, but if you are both doing radically different things in an area or have radically different thoughts, then you have the opportunity for a massive idea.

Simply, we compare what you do with your leadership to what your massive idea partner does for his leadership and see if there is an opportunity for a massive idea in the differences of what you each do or different perspective. Then repeat this process for each area of your business. Now keep in mind that your Inner Circle Massive Idea Partners can still bring ideas to the table, their perspective is different than yours and they may have had life experiences or previous work experiences that lead to a Massive Growth Idea.

Massive Growth Ideas are judged based on how much profit they can provide your business, not just top line income. It will do you no good to grow your business by 41 million dollars if it costs $1 million dollars to grow. That's breaking even and will not get you to your dreams. We want massive profit in these growth ideas. There are two ways to grow profits, either increase your income or reduce your costs. You grow your business massively by increasing your sales or substantially reducing your costs.

Now, maybe what you're thinking is that you need to find really huge ideas right away. You don't. You can find massive ideas in your business even with lots of really small ideas because everything adds up. Small ideas accumulate into one massive strategy in many cases rather than one great idea in only one area of your business. There's a multiplicative effect when we do it this way and we'll show you exactly what that means when we get into the examples, but just know that you can even have lots of small ideas that result in massive growth. It's time to start digging.

So, to get through all the crap and to the massive idea we need to set the stage of the conversation that you're going to have with your Massive Idea partner by structuring the conversation and using some very powerful and focused questions about each of the 6 Massive Growth Areas (Leadership, Management, Financial, Marketing, Sales and Production). Questions that are going to get both you and your Massive Idea Partner thinking in a different way. If this person in your Outer Circle you will need to give them a brief overview of what you are currently doing in each of the 6 Massive Growth Areas.

6 Massive Growth Areas

Leadership – This is the CEO and above such as your Board of Directors and/or Advisors. This is the group of people that provide the vision of your company. Maybe it's you and your spouse that run your business, you guys are the leadership, and the systems that manage this part of your business.

Management - Corporate offices such as VP's and below, including all employees, and the systems that manage this part of your business. This is the management of the business and remember this is not a clear concise cut line in the sand that you can't cross.

Financial- Corporate offices such as VP's and below, including all employees, and the systems that manage this part of your business, anything dealing with the finances, sometimes this also involves your infrastructure, your IT structure, that can also be considered financial, whatever you consider but just think about your business from a different angle.

Marketing - Corporate offices such as VP's and below, including all employees, and the systems that manage this part of your business. Anything that you used to create interest in your product or service so that your sales team can take over and actually close the sale. This is your advertising. This is brochures, this is billboards, radio TV, whatever kind of way to use to generate and gain new client leads and then your sales team closes them in their conversion process

Sales - Corporate offices such as VP's and below, including all of your employees, and the systems that manage this part of your business. Sales staff, sales managers, events, vehicles, uniforms, scripts, training, etc.

Production – Corporate offices such as VP's and below, including all of your employees, and the systems that manage this part of your business. Equipment, design, product development, research and development.

To Start The Conversation

You will need to tell your Massive Idea Partner what your leadership vision is, in a nutshell this is your elevator pitch. For example, when we talked to Marcus Lemonis about our business this is what we told him. That, as the owners, we envisioned helping other small business grow to the next level, through marketing and sales efforts. When he asked how we were currently doing this we explained that we were marketing to lists and Sam was calling them and closing them on our marketing services. As we explained this in detail, telling Marcus that as a way to close them on the phone, was to make some connections to other customers in our network and giving them ideas for them to grow. After about a 30-minute conversation and Marcus, who was part of our Outer Circle, he identified part of our Massive Growth Idea. He said, "You guys are facilitators" you bring entrepreneurs connections to other people and resources in a massive way, giving them the opportunity for massive growth." And then there was our Aha moment…our Massive Growth Idea, or at least the Leadership part of the idea. There were a lot more parts to this idea that we had to figure out and that would come as we discussed the other 5 areas of our business with other Massive Idea Partners.

To help you find your Massive Growth Idea you need to ask the following questions for the 6 Massive Growth Areas of your business.

1. How can my Massive Idea Partner's [Leadership, Management, Financial, Marketing, Sales, Production] system/skills/resources improve my product/service and make them more valuable?

2. How can my Massive Idea Partner's [Leadership, Management, Financial, Marketing, Sales, Production] system/skills/resources make my customer/clients more valuable?

3. How can my Massive Idea Partner's [Leadership, Management, Financial, Marketing, Sales, Production] system/skills/resources give my business a brand-new product/service?

4. How can my Massive Idea Partner's [Leadership, Management, Financial, Marketing, Sales, Production] system/skills/resources give me a new customer/client?

Below, we put together what we call a Massive Idea Generator worksheet to give you a jumpstart on your brainstorming session so that you have a little head start with the conversation to help you find the Massive Growth Idea. This will give you a whole bunch of things to look at.

You and your Massive Idea Partner will look at your business and see how they would improve your product or service? Would they give you give new customers or clients? Would they increase your sales, reduce cost, technology, changing packaging, all these different things?

You and your Massive Idea Partner should look at this idea generator and get your juices flowing and then look at your company as all of these ideas could be massive Growth Opportunities. An added benefit to your Massive Idea Partner is that it will help them to come up with their own Massive Growth Idea too, this works both ways. For now we'll focus on the advantages you'll get by doing this but quite honestly your Massive Idea Partner will benefit just as much from this exercise as you will.

You're Only One Idea Away From Massive Business Growth
Go to www.TheDrivingForceBook.com to get Your FREE Gift Worth $747.83

Idea Generator

New/Customer/Client Ideas

Existing Customer/Client Ideas

Increase Sales for Your Company

Reduce Costs for Your Company

Technology

Changing Packaging

Better Sales Processes

Better Sales Capabilities

Better Marketing Processes

Better Marketing Capabilities

Adding New Services

Economies of Scale – Better Pricing

Incorporating New Components/Services In the Product

More Product Options

Changing the Marketing Message

Increasing Marketing Channels

Sources for Important Resources

Connections with other people

So, let's start asking the questions to get you to your Massive Growth Idea.

The Driving Force Massive
Business Growth Formula

Leadership

1. How can my Massive Idea Partner's Leadership system improve my product or service and make them more valuable?

   _____
   _____

2. How can my Massive Idea Partner's Leadership system or skills or resources make my customer or clients more valuable?

   _____
   _____

3. Massive Idea Partner's Leadership system or skills or resources give my business a brand-new product or service?

   _____
   _____

4. Massive Idea Partner's Leadership system or skills or resources give me a new customer or client?

   _____
   _____

You're Only One Idea Away From Massive Business Growth
Go to www.TheDrivingForceBook.com to get Your FREE Gift Worth $747.83

Management

5. How can my Massive Idea Partner's Management system improve my product or service and make them more valuable?

_____
_____

6. How can my Massive Idea Partner's Management system or skills or resources make my customer or clients more valuable?

_____
_____

7. Massive Idea Partner's Management system or skills or resources give my business a brand-new product or service?

_____
_____

8. Massive Idea Partner's Management system or skills or resources give me a new customer or client?

_____
_____

Financial

9. How can my Massive Idea Partner's Financial system improve my product or service and make them more valuable?

   _____
   _____

10. How can my Massive Idea Partner's Financial system or skills or resources make my customer or clients more valuable?

    _____
    _____

11. Massive Idea Partner's Financial system or skills or resources give my business a brand-new product or service?

    _____
    _____

12. Massive Idea Partner's Financial system or skills or resources give me a new customer or client?

    _____
    _____

Marketing

13. How can my Massive Idea Partner's Marketing system improve my product or service and make them more valuable?

_____

_____

14. How can my Massive Idea Partner's Marketing system or skills or resources make my customer or clients more valuable?

_____

_____

15. Massive Idea Partner's Marketing system or skills or resources give my business a brand-new product or service?

_____

_____

16. Massive Idea Partner's Marketing system or skills or resources give me a new customer or client?

_____

_____

The Driving Force Massive
Business Growth Formula

Sales

17. How can my Massive Idea Partner's Sales system improve my product or service and make them more valuable?

   _____
   _____

18. How can my Massive Idea Partner's Sales system or skills or resources make my customer or clients more valuable?

   _____
   _____

19. Massive Idea Partner's Sales system or skills or resources give my business a brand-new product or service?

   _____
   _____

20. Massive Idea Partner's Sales system or skills or resources give me a new customer or client?

   _____
   _____

Production

21. How can my Massive Idea Partner's Production system improve my product or service and make them more valuable?

   _____
   _____

22. How can my Massive Idea Partner's Production system or skills or resources make my customer or clients more valuable?

   _____
   _____

23. Massive Idea Partner's Production system or skills or resources give my business a brand-new product or service?

   _____
   _____

24. Massive Idea Partner's Production system or skills or resources give me a new customer or client?

   _____
   _____

Putting It All Together

25. Now take all of your ideas and summarize your Massive Growth Idea and all of the parts of your business that you'll need to put it together to make sure that it will happen as quickly as possible.

_____
_____
_____
_____
_____
_____
_____
_____
_____
_____

This Works in Any Industry

Jim and Cathy (not their real names) are current members of the Driving Force Mastermind. A midwestern couple that started a business teaching K through 12 kids how to read. Over many decades their business expanded and they expanded their service offerings many times. Now offering a new summer camp, a new tutoring program in many educational areas including one on one tutoring and then even focusing on children with special needs and those with more difficult disciplinary concerns.

Jim and Cathy have been around the block a few times and paid heavily many times for consultants, coaches, training programs, advisors and experts to help them grow their business in many different ways. They pay many thousands of dollars a month for someone to handle their social media, many thousands of dollars a year for a monthly mastermind group, hundreds of dollars an hour to speak to a consultant on a weekly basis. They had invested a couple thousand dollars at a time for various trainings and marketing programs and participated in product launches and bought into many a guru's programs.

Jim and Cathy work hard for every dollar they earn in their business and treat each dollar spent as an investment into their future, so with every dollar they spend they expect a return on that investment. And they worked hard at it, not the typical attitude of inaction that so many follow. They didn't do the typical buy it and let it collect dust on the shelf, as so many do. They followed the advice of every consultant. The took action and did, to the best of their ability, exactly as directed to maximize their results. They completed the trainings that they had spent thousands on, they filled out the worksheets and implemented the lessons.

And they got results. Not great results, but their actions did produce some results, some small results, some lackluster results. They spent years and years with these types of programs along with many, many thousands of dollars and countless hours. And if they had continued to follow this path they would have grown their business at a little less than the national average of 7.5% per year. Some years were good, some years weren't as good.

Reluctantly, at first, they gave the Driving Force process a try. Step 1 was completed even before they signed up. They truly decided that enough was enough and wanted to grow in a massive way. After years and years of frustratingly slow growth, not even matching the national average, they were ready for a change, ready for something big to come along and propel them and their business forward.

Then a week or so later Step 2 broke them through a major barrier to their growth. The stifling barrier of slow growth was not that they didn't have great services, it wasn't that they weren't following the direction that their advisors and training had recommended. What was stifling their massive growth was that all of the paths of growth that they had pursued in the past were small ideas, with small goals and so only achieved small results. It wasn't until they started to think in the ways of massive growth that a Massive Growth Idea was able to reveal itself to them.

Jim and Cathy had always thought regionally about their services and it wasn't until they asked themselves and their Massive Idea Partners these powerful 24 questions that they realized that their growth was limited by their potential client base size. When they looked at a much larger pool of clients the potential growth was magnified by over 1000%. When their idea expanded to a national level versus a regional level their big idea became clear. It was like the clouds parted and the sun shone through after a thunderstorm. Their Massive Growth Idea opened up an entirely new strategy for massive forward momentum.

Jim and Cathy were going to take their reading program and convert it to an electronic delivery training program using their proprietary teaching method. They realized that even though there were going to be some major obstacles, that the growth potential with a national customer base was the only way for them to take their passion for helping the millions (yes millions) of illiterate children to finally learn how to read and growth their business in massive ways.

Now every idea is riddled with obstacles and problems to be overcome, but the idea must be the starting place and it must be a big idea so that it's worth the pursuit of the answers to the problems that will inevitably be encountered along the way.

So, they moved into Massive Action Mode and connected with the right people and right resources as you'll discover moving forward. But it all starts with the Massive Growth Idea and with the help of your Massive Idea Partners you can have your own breakthrough idea very quickly. Ask the questions, use the idea generator and fill out the worksheet, what have you got to lose and most importantly what have you got to gain?

Chapter 6

Massive Action Mode

The Driving Force Massive
Business Growth Formula

Step Three

Empty Your Cup

(A favorite story from Walter Bergeron)

One of my favorite stories concerns a Buddhist student and a Zen Master. The student asked the master to teach him. Then, he began to talk about his extensive knowledge and background and rambled on and on about all of the previous studies he had done on this subject. So, the master listened patiently and then began to make tea. When it was ready, he poured the tea into the student's cup until it began to overflow and run all over the floor. Then the student saw what was happening and shouted, "Stop, stop! The cup is full; you can't get anymore in."

The master stopped pouring and said: "You are like this cup; you are full of ideas and previous knowledge. You come and ask for teaching, but your cup is full; I can't put anything in. Before I can teach you, you'll have to empty your cup."

This story is an old one, and you've probably heard it before but it's especially important for this course because, before I can show you any new and exciting concepts on how to take your business and really grow it, I am going to ask you to empty your cup, at least for the duration of this course. To take in this new knowledge and make it your own you'll have to open your mind and instead of dismissing any of what you are about to be revealed as, not applicable to you or your business, instead give consideration to how you can apply it to your business and your personal situation.

So, to begin this part of the Driving Force process I need you to forget whatever it is you already think you know about massive growth in your business. Empty your cup because we are going to fill it with a completely new way for you to think about how you are going to be able to extract the most growth from your business.

Set Up a Massive Action Work Environment

This book is as much about the information as it is about implementation, so in order to get the most out of this I want you to set up a massive action work environment. So set aside time to complete each exercise in this book, even if that means that you must make an appointment with yourself or with your team to make sure this time gets set aside. If you are completing these exercises with a team set aside time for each of you to work independently and then time for you to work together on creating a shared vision. Don't worry about making this look pretty and perfect or use exact words or get all the details just right. This is about massive action resulting in massive implementation.

Massive Action Work Environment Checklist:

- ✓ Find a quiet room where you won't be disturbed
- ✓ Put a Do Not Disturb sign on the door, then close it and lock it
- ✓ Put phone on do not disturb or just unplug it
- ✓ Turn off you cell phone
- ✓ Turn off your email
- ✓ Turn off any instant messaging or chat features
- ✓ Close out of all programs except the one you are using to complete this exercise

3 Golden Nuggets of Massive Action

One - Take Massive Action Every Single Day

This was huge. I did this by taking an 11 x 17 sheet of paper and taping it to the wall near my desk so I would see it every single time I went into my office. I knew that if I continued to take "baby steps" then I would get "baby results" and that was simply unacceptable any longer. Massive action meant that I would also probably make massive mistakes and make a massive fool of myself – SO WHAT! I was the CEO, The President of the company and if it took me making huge errors and making myself look stupid then that was exactly what I was going to do and so that is exactly what I did.

I had to first get myself a work environment that allowed me the time and privacy I needed. So my first act of massive action was to put signs up on my office door and even along the walls to my office. "GO AWAY", "YES I DO BITE", "IF THERE IS A FIRE – PUT IT OUT", "IF THERE IS AN EMERGENCY DIAL 911", "LEAVE ME ALONE"

And hey, they worked. I was left undisturbed most of the time and my staff adjusted quickly by simply emailing me from the next office down the hall and I took care of things when I would take breaks.

After a few weeks my staff would start to ignore the signs, but I was just as determined to keep the work environment as productive as possible, so I had to take massive action again.

This may seem irrelevant but follow me on this. I was born on Halloween, yep October 31st, and so this holiday has always meant a great deal to me. I dress up in a costume every year, and yes even now I dress up and we throw a BIG Halloween/Birthday party. Over the years my wife has taken this to a whole new level. We now go shopping in August and start to prepare for the big party. She has accumulated 10 pallets, yes 10 forklift sized pallets of Halloween decorations. 6 foot wide by 6 foot tall by 8 foot high pallets of every imaginable Halloween decoration including 8 life sized animated horror movie props. One of those animated props is Michael Meyers, of the famed Halloween movies. So back to my massive action.

Hockey mask on and knife in hand, I placed Michael Meyers just outside my office door with those signs taped all over him to "STAY AWAY", "OWNER BITES REALLY HARD" and wouldn't you know it, it worked again. Everyone left me alone so I could continue my trek into ,massive growth implementation.

I also realized that 5 days a week was not enough, even during the weekends my mind would be racing with ideas and enthusiasm about the marketing ideas from the week. I would wake up on Saturday mornings with these thoughts, but by Monday they would be gone. So I took massive action again and started waking up an hour earlier than the rest of the household, sit at my laptop with a cup of "Joe" and I would write sales letters, and make revisions to copy and sometimes just THINK. In the peace of the early morning before the sun had come up I would just think and dream of what I am accomplishing and make it real in my mind, that the reality of success had already happened and I was living the life I imagined. And then I would get right back at it with an all new vigor.

So if you ever have an excuse that your staff won't leave you alone or you just can't find the time. You just need to dig a little deeper and find a more creative and totally extreme way to MAKE that time. MAKE it happen. MAKE it massive every single day.

Two - Good Is Good Enough

This part of Massive Action Mode may be a little hard to swallow. It was for me too. I am an engineer by trade and for years and years, PERFECTION was good enough. Pursuit of perfection and only your best was good enough, were the mantra's I lived by. "If it ain't your best, then it ain't ready to send to your clients" that is what I pounded into my skull year after year. So this new philosophy of good is good enough is a real tough one to overcome.

As I moved forward massively growing my business, a new mantra sprung forth, and I decided that "The third time is a charm" would be my good is good enough measuring stick or mantra. I would work on something and give myself 3 revisions, then I would send it out the door to my clients. If I couldn't make it perfect after 3 tries, then so be it, errors and all were going out the door and I would just have to make corrections after the fact, when and if they ever were needed. This book is a perfect example of that. There are errors, there are things that could be worded better and more eloquently but after 3 tries, I am sending this to be published and I'll fix errors later but I am getting this thing out the door right away and not looking back wishing I had done a better job. A good book published is significantly better than a perfect book unpublished.

Three - Simultaneous Implementation

This part Massive Action Mode seems to defy physics, you can only do one thing at a time. You can only be in one place at a time and it is physically impossible to do anything other than one thing at a time. Well, that is in essence a correct assumption but what I wanted to do was to get a task completed up to a point that I could simply go no further. What that meant to me was for example...

When I started my newsletters. I would do as much as I could as fast as I could and then I would hit a roadblock. Sometimes I would simply run out of ideas, sometimes my eyes would start to cross because I had been staring at the computer screen far too long or sometimes I just got bored with what I was doing. So I would then stop go take care of something in the office, or put stamps on envelopes or go fold some long form sales letters or some other task that would move me forward, onto something that gave me more satisfaction and that I could make more progress on. I would come back to the newsletters after a couple of hours and finish them up but at the end of the day I had two or three implemented strategies and that made multiple things happen at the same time. I did this every day and then as different projects took different timeframes to complete after a couple of weeks it was like every day something new was being completed and getting fully implemented. That fueled my enthusiasm so I worked even harder to make that happen again. I got a little drunk on accomplishment and I liked it, so I did it even more.

One - Take Massive Action Every Single Day
Two - Good Is Good Enough
Three - Simultaneous Implementation

Chapter 7

Connect Your Idea To Extraordinary People

Step Four

Now I don't mean necessarily celebrities like Marcus Lemonis, there are many other types of extraordinary people that can be of massive value to you. I also don't mean somebody that has superhuman powers. What I do mean is someone that has extraordinary, even unusual or remarkable knowledge, experience or strength in any one of those six business areas that we just talked about, or someone that has remarkable knowledge, experience or strength in any of those ideas that you wrote down.

We have actually clients in our Mastermind Group right now, who are connected to the guys who marketed and made the George Foreman Grill so popular. These are the Cesari Brothers, Rick and Steve Cesari, and they're responsible for taking this taco shell-maker and turned it into the famous George Foreman Grill. These are the guys who are responsible for finding George Foreman, they are responsible for putting it online, for making this thing a massive sales, multi-billion dollar success, and then eventually George got very, very wealthy off of it, even more so than when he was the heavyweight champion of the world in boxing.

But these guys are not movie or even TV celebrities, they possess skills much more valuable and do have extraordinary gifts, extraordinary experience strength and knowledge. Their extraordinary skills are in national direct marketing, national direct brand marketing.

One of our Driving Force mastermind members discovered (Jim and Cathy) their massive growth idea. They were going to launch their children's reading program on a national level, but they did not have the extraordinary connections they needed to do this. So, we were able to facilitate an extraordinary connection with Rick and Steve Cesari. That one extraordinary connection has enabled them to take their educational services product out to a national level. That's the power of connecting the right people to the right idea. They were able to go through this process to come up with a massive idea for their business and then connect that idea to some extraordinary people that knew how to take that idea to a massive level by finding the right people, the right extraordinary people that have remarkable knowledge, experience, and strength.

You can't take your massive idea and make it suddenly become a reality in a vacuum. You're going to have to connect to the right people and make this thing happen.

How to Discover Who Your Extraordinary Connections Need to be

To find out for yourself who the right extraordinary connections are to help you achieve your massive goals with your massive idea you need to ask yourself these questions.

Who can make more money than you can from your products?

_____

_____

This is where you look far and wide to find companies with the capacity to scale your products or services into much larger markets. This would be an extraordinary connection that can easily introduce your products or services into existing customers and/or existing distribution channels. This extraordinary connection has the capacity and the muscle to rapidly expand your products into an industry you are not currently in. Think of as many as you can and write them down.

Who can remove a constraint on your business?

_____

_____

If you want to exponentially grow your business by at least 10 times, what are the one or two road blocks constraining your ability to do that? This could be location, distribution channel, export capability, finances and so on. If the constraint could be removed, how much more revenue and profit could you achieve. Your extraordinary connection is the connection that can instantly overcome your road blocks.

Who has a problem you can fix?

_____

_____

Your extraordinary connection may lack the capability or capacity in a new area, new technology or new process. Sometimes the quickest way to make an extraordinary connection is to help them first.

What threat can you reduce or eliminate?

_____

_____

A threat occurs when a company or industry has a potential or actual decline in current revenue. Maybe from an existing or new competitor.

They may not have the luxury of time to create a competitive product and so acquiring already available products may help to eliminate or reduce the threat. A threat may also occur where the competitors are anticipated to undertake some action.

Being first off the block may counter the advantage they otherwise would achieve. A threat may also come with loss of a key distribution agreement, key account or key capability. Loss of key staff may create a gap in capability in any part of the company.

This is when an extraordinary connection could be used to resolve the problem as well as provide increased capability. So, if you can eliminate a threat to a product or service, that becomes a potential extraordinary connection for you.

Who sells to the same customers you sell to?

_____

_____

Scanning customers to find another company which sells to them will often indicate a potential extraordinary connection who can capitalize on knowledge of that type of customer. They may be able to cross sell products or utilize their own distribution channel to move new products.

Who uses the same technology you use?

_____

_____

If a key ingredient to the success of your company is the use of a specific technology which is expensive or difficult or time consuming to acquire, another company that uses that technology may want to connect to another company to increase capacity or enter new markets.

Who needs your customer base?

_____

_____

The customer base can often be a very valuable asset, especially if it provides opportunities for the extraordinary connection to sell additional products or to break into a new sector. Also, think about who needs your marketing capabilities.

Who needs your technology or people?

_____

_____

If you have a specialized technology, especially if protected with patents, or specialized staff with deep knowledge, this can provide an extraordinary connection with huge scalable opportunities.

Now that you have a list of possible potential extraordinary connections that you've thought of on your own, I want you to answer those very same questions in a mastermind setting and have your mastermind partners help you come up with even more answers for extraordinary connections.

In case you are not familiar with the concept of masterminds let us run down some of the other secret gems of how you can reap the benefits of allowing others to help you to achieve massive growth with the transformational experience of a mastermind.

Don't Be the Smartest Person in the Room

Now this may sound counterintuitive. When you are among your peers it sure feels good to be the sharpest tack in the bunch, but when in a mastermind, this can be a great disadvantage to you. You should seek out groups that have members that are exceedingly more successful than you are. Take a shot and apply for membership into a group that has members that are way out of your league. Your growth will come from stretching your reach and becoming involved with those that have done far more than you. You could gain unfettered access to input from some of the best and the brightest in an industry and this is the one of the fastest ways to grow yourself and your business. We've both done this and found ourselves in a room with just such a group of people. For example, if you had access to a group that had members that had businesses 20 times your size, maybe another member is considered a genuine Guru of sales presentations, and yet another is considered a direct mail Guru that had done billions of mailings and others had bought and sold many businesses. The vast experience of such a group will prove invaluable, as every time you meet and your issues change, someone will have experience and help you to find a solution.

Do Individual Hot Seats

Now if you have never been a part of a hot seat style mastermind, this is when you put yourself in the front of a room and pour your problems out to a group of strangers. Then they drill in on the root cause of your issues and make suggestions for solutions or generate ideas that you might never have considered. This is a tremendously powerful, although frequently intimidating, exercise and is ultimately one of the most compelling reasons to get involved with a mastermind. When a group of top notch entrepreneurs has 40 plus minutes to focus in on your needs and bounce ideas off of you as well as each other, the solutions can be fast and furious not to mention radically unexpected and life changing. Such transformations happen often, we just recently had one of our members asking for help on a new business idea he had just started to work on. During the first 10 minutes of his hot seat the group fired back at him that this was a terrible idea and had been proven to be a flawed concept by multiple other larger and more adept businesses. This of course was not what the member expected to hear. A couple of months later he came back to the group and reported that he had done more research and took the advice of the group. He stated that his hotseat likely saved him hundreds of thousands of dollars and many years of frustrating failure had he moved forward with his idea and not consulted the group first.

Do Your Homework

Make sure you are ready for the group when you go in. Have your questions ready for the group by picking one or two top issues you want help with. This will give the group the ability to focus on your most important issues and allow them time to ask questions and give input.

Having too many questions will diminish the groups' ability to help you and you won't get as much out of the time you have available. You will also need to know the relevant numbers that deal with your question, especially when it comes to sales and marketing. You'll need to know things like sales volume, conversion rates, ROI, Cost per lead, etc.. Without these numbers and details you will only be able to get partial answers and you'll go away with more things to test or data to compile than you will with ideas to implement and solutions to the core issues you brought to the group.

Take a Day Off

Don't go back to work right away, take one or two days off after the event to allow your mind to process what has happened and ponder the solutions. This time to decompress and process will be immensely enhanced by journaling your thoughts. Write down the ideas that come to mind, this will pay you huge dividends. You will feel more rested, your thoughts and ideas will be freshly documented and your mind will have had more time to offer you a better solution.

Record Every Word of It

With rapid fire answers, recommendations and guidance from so many people, there will be no way for you to remember everything everyone said to you in detail. So record the entire conversation, just be aware that others may edit what they say when they are told that they are being recorded.

Pay For It

You get what you pay for, you also get back the same amount of effort you put into something. Masterminds are no exception to these time tested facts. When there is a sacrifice or a substantial cost to membership you will find that you put much more effort into the group as well as demand better solutions from it. When I found myself writing that very large check for my masterminds, it made me demand results from the participation I put into the group as well as I would not settle for mediocre solutions from anyone. Feeling the pain of knowing that the cost was substantial, produced results many times more valuable than the cost of the membership. You will find that if there is no cost or sacrifice then you won't care that you don't get results or solutions and you will have no incentive to get the most out of the group and you will certainly not put your best effort into the group.

Get Uncomfortable

Part of the power of the mastermind is to stretch your mind to what else is possible and you can do that more easily when you are not in a familiar place. Travelling will force you out of your comfort zone and put your mind into a state that will more readily accept alternative suggestions and different input from others. You will need to communicate what you are thinking and reveal things about yourself and your business that are uncomfortable, leaving you feeling vulnerable and exposed, but this is where the breakthroughs happen. If you keep yourself guarded and you won't let others in to help you, then you are wasting the resources of this powerful group dynamic.

Chapter 8

Connect Your Idea To Extraordinary Resources

Step Five

The next piece you are going to need in your journey to implement your massive idea are resources. Resources such as time, money, lists, skills, people, vendors, etc.. Earlier we talked about our Mastermind Group members Jim and Cathy, they had the idea to take their children's reading program and then connected to Rick and Steve Cesari, they also needed money in order to pay for completing the high-end video production as well as paying for national marketing media. They got the massive growth idea, they went outside their industry and they came up with this, then they connected to the right people, and they now needed the right resources.

The Resources You're Going To Need

There may be many resources you'll need along the way to turn your massive idea into reality, so let's brainstorm and list out of all those needs right now.

You're Only One Idea Away From Massive Business Growth
Go to www.TheDrivingForceBook.com to get Your FREE Gift Worth $747.83

1. **Money** – How much will you need? When will you need it?

   _____

   _____

2. **Lists** – Will you need more leads to feed into your marketing and sales funnel? Who are they? How many lists of leads will you possibly need? Give details here.

   _____

   _____

3. **Outsourcing** – Can you turn over specific functions to a third party provider to implement and support, for a fee?

   _____

   _____

4. **Joint Ventures** – Do you need any strategic alliances where two or more parties form a partnership to share markets, assets, knowledge, and, of course, profits?

   _____

   _____

5. **Affiliates** – Do you need a type of re-seller arrangement where the affiliate refers customers and is rewarded financially for doing so?

_____
_____

6. **Technology** – Do you need to use other people's technology to cut overheads, streamline operations, access new markets, support remote workers etc?

_____
_____

7. **Systems** – Will you need new systematizing of any of your business functions so that they operate with the least amount of human intervention?

_____
_____

8. **Exchanging Services** – You will need to be able to barter your services with those of another person or company for mutual benefit. This will reduce the amount of money you may need. Which services can you use for bartering to reach your massive idea?

_____
_____

9. **Mastermind Groups** – You will need to regularly connect with and exploit the talents, contacts, ideas, experience, intelligence etc. of like-minded peers. Which groups will you be a part of?

_____
_____

10. **Other** – What other needs do you feel will be absolutely crucial to achieve your Massive Growth Idea?

_____
_____

Negotiating to Get the Best Deal for Your Resources

To make sure you get the most benefit from your extraordinary resources, you'll need to prepare for any negotiations with your new vendor or investor. You'll need to put yourself in their shoes and take their position as a new perspective so that you can know what's going on both as the buyer and a seller of this resource. There are a lot of reasons that this is really important and yet it's something that's so often neglected.

Our mastermind member taking their reading program to a national level had a need for new resources, they needed money. They had to produce this product on a national scale. If there's a hit they need to be able to produce many, many, many of them very, very quickly. They need money for production of the video, money for production of the actual product, the CDs, DVDs, whatever else, all the stuff that goes into it, but they needed money. They needed other resources other than just people. And they will have to purchase this money. They'll pay for it with equity in their business or in the form of interest on a loan or even a barter for some type of extraordinary service they can provide. But make no mistake that they will have to be a buyer of these resources.

Connecting to extraordinary resources is the next step in this massive growth process. These resources actually help that dream, that big growth idea come into fruition. They needed actually a capital, they needed money. We were actually able to facilitate them getting in touch with a private investor, who funded the entire growth of their business, actually non-equity investor, which was fantastic for them. Someone else was going to put up the money, wanting a good return but didn't necessarily want any control of their company. They were able to take it on a massive growth.

We, as buyers of services or resources tend to think of everything in terms of "I." That it's all about my business and what I want and what I want to accomplish. While that's very important and probably the place you want to start with, it's certainly not the place you want to end with. It's not the only position, the only viewpoint that you want to have when you're thinking about how to get the resources you'll need from your vendor in order to implement your massive growth idea. You want to be able to communicate to them in a way that speaks their language, not just your language.

When we start out, we always start off with what our needs are as buyers, but when we get to the point where we want to be a little more advanced, when we want to communicate effectively with the resource provider, we want to know what they're thinking first and foremost and be able to have a great conversation with them.

There are two sides of the table when it comes to growing your business through the resources of others, and you really and truly you want to know what's going on in detail on both sides of that table for two big reasons.

Know What Their Needs Are First

One reason comes from the point of being able to negotiate with the resource provider because there are going to be pricing terms spoken about, timeframe that you have to stay in a relationship with them and all sorts of things that are going to go into the negotiations of the resources you need for your business.

You want to be able to do that effectively, and a way to do that effectively is to know, before the negotiations what their questions or concerns will be and you want to be able to have a response. The only way to know that is to be able to speak from both sides of the table. The other reason being familiar with both sides of the negotiations table is that during this process you will really need to convey emotion from your side, your perspective, to the other person's perspective. To convey emotion effectively you'll need to know where they are emotionally, know what they're thinking about. That is absolutely crucial.

I'm going to go through a few different ways to make sure that you're prepared and know exactly how to be on both sides of this negotiation table or at least have the idea that you'll be able to consider the perspective of the other side of the table because it's so important.

Understand the Resource You Want Access To

One reason is because, well quite frankly, you'll be able to answer questions a whole lot easier when they come up. We were in negotiations not too long ago with an HVAC company, and the owner was using the extraordinary resources of a really large landscaping company. They both shared the common ground of having the same type of customers. They both served the homeowner. Both sides of the negotiation table had a lot of things in common. They could really speak the same language because they knew who their customers were, but when it came to pricing, they really had no idea what the pricing structure was of each other.

So, when the question came up about what is the value of a customer there were problems. To an HVAC customer, it was fairly high on the front end of the transaction. It was $20,000 initially for an HVAC company because the typical initial purchase was a brand-new replacement unit. Now for a landscaping company, in most cases, the initial purchase was a monthly continuity membership where they're being charged $300 per month. Initially, the landscaping company said that the value of each client per month was very, very low, and they didn't understand why this question was so important. To the HVAC company the reason it was so important was because they wanted to determine just how long they kept their customers for.

A landscaping customer keeps their customers for a long time, and it's a service they provide on a monthly basis. The HVAC company focused primarily on a one-time sale, and then never properly communicated with their customers, which was one reason why the landscaper wanted them, because they had very, very high value customers. Knowing where each buyer and seller is coming from, understanding the language, understanding the questions that are going to come up will be really important for the buyer of these resources. The HVAC company really understood, almost second nature, exactly what questions to ask, before the landscaping company could even ask them.

Understanding what you're the business of your opponent is important, especially when it comes to questions that are going to be asked. Knowing the other person's business, knowing how they speak and the language that their customers talk in and the terminology of what they do, that's really important to negotiations. Knowing that definitely helps answer questions way before they come up and prepares you a whole lot better for when those questions do come up. Make sure that you have the perspective of being on both sides of the table, especially when it comes to questions, so that you can fully understand the resource you are about to get involved with.

Understanding Price Resources

Another reason you want to do this is that one of the biggest questions that usually comes up is the price for a service. Well, we as entrepreneurs, of course we want the most we can get for our services so your resource provider will want to get the maximum amount by asking for a high price for their resource. But the most important questions should not be about price, they should be about value and other services that can be offered to offset the cost and enhance the value for any service you pay for.

Just recently I (Walter Bergeron) had some large trees trimmed and a couple of them removed in the back property near my home. When the guy came to remove the trees, he gave me a quote. When he came to give me the quote to remove the trees and to do the trimming, I didn't know what questions to ask. Like most customers, I had no idea what he was going to do. All I knew was that when he left, I was hoping I wouldn't have to cleanup a bunch of mess and the tree limbs that were blocking the fence and the property would be gone and the trees that I wanted removed, they'd be gone too, and I wouldn't be left with a big stump in the middle of my yard.

That's kind of what I assumed. I assumed I'd have a big mess with leaves all over the place, and a big stump stuck there that I'd have to cut around or slowly chop with a saw or something to get rid of. I just didn't know what to expect. When he got there to give me a quote, he started to explain a little bit of what they were going to do and then he stopped. All he told me was, "Yeah, we'll pick it all up for you. You'll have a nice, clean yard. We'll get rid of the stump for you, and we'll leave you a nice, clean place." Then nothing. A stopping point in the conversation and I guess what he wanted was me to say yes and pay him, but it just didn't feel right. I felt like there should be more conversation so I went into the only thing I knew that I could ask and that was price. So, I did what everyone else does that doesn't know what else to ask about and I said, "How much is this going to cost?" He said something like $1,800 or $2,000, whatever the quote was, depending on if they had to clean it up or what I wanted, if I wanted to keep some of it for firewood or something. The conversation pretty much stopped there, and he left. Then, another landscaping company came to give me another quote, and what they did is they started asking me a bunch of questions. He knew what my issues were going to be before I even asked them. He started asking me questions,

"Well, would you like to keep some of it for firewood?" I said, "Well, sure. Would it save me on price?" "Oh, yes sir. It will save you on price, but here's a better option."

The Conversation Will Turn to Price

It turns out after this conversation was over, because he asked all the right questions, not only did I get his landscaping services, I also bought firewood from the guy, which is another business he owned. I also wound up having him come and cut my lawn every single month because he was a really good salesperson, and had other conversations for me to have. We never really discussed price because we kept talking about solutions for me as a homeowner. That's the same thing you want to do as business seller. You would not like to let the buyer run out of conversation and then jump to price right when you first start having these conversations. The best thing you can do to avoid this kind of issue is to know what's going to happen on the other side of the table.

Know that as soon as you run out of conversations that lean towards solutions for the buyer, that he's going to start asking you about price. Now, you will have to handle that price question at some point and you'll know the answer.

What I don't want you to do is, I don't want you to have to have that conversation right away. Before you have the price conversation, you should have already had so many other questions and solutions and value built up, because you know what they're going to ask and know what their needs are before they even ask these questions. As you know, if you ever have a salesperson that works for you, you know that a good salesperson knows the objections that are going to come up before the customer even has them. You know that your best salespeople are not somebody that knows your product the best, your best salespeople are your salespeople who know your customer the best, who know what they're going to think before they even ask it. They know both sides of this table, this negotiation table so well, it makes it easy for them because they know what's going to happen, they know the reasons customers don't buy or have objections.

Know the Objections Before They Bring Them Up

You really need to get into the mind of their business, because by knowing that you'll know what questions come up first, you'll be able to handle those objections. You should not have to address price right away during a conversation, you should be addressing value and solutions during the initial parts of this conversation. That's why it's so important to do that. It's a really powerful place to be. It's really powerful to be able to handle objections before they come up or when they do come up from the buyer you have an answer right away, rather than the thing that most sellers do is when a tough question is asked, they have to either stumble through an answer, make one up on the spot or say something like, "I'll have to get back to you on that."

When that happens, that tells the buyer that you really don't know what you're talking about. Those things will come up, it's not like you're going to totally avoid those. If you were to think about what the buyer's needs were before that conversation was there, step into his shoes before he even came to the negotiation table or had the phone call where you guys are starting to discuss some pricing. If you knew those answers in the front end because you did your homework, it would be a whole lot more smooth conversation and it actually helps the negotiations and the sales process move along a whole lot faster and a whole lot easier.

We start this with knowing what the buyer needs, what solutions he needs so that you have those solutions at hand, ready to give to him at a moment's notice whenever those questions come up. That's really powerful when it comes to doing this. What happens if you don't do this? What happens if you don't do your homework and don't understand what the buyer wants before they come to the table? Well, it puts you in a position where you become a lot more exposed. When you have to answer questions with, "I don't know" or "I'll get back to you" or worse case, you just make something up and give them some BS answer because you want to continue the conversation, you expose yourself because during these conversations, these are actually legal conversations where you can be bound to your answers. Be careful with that. Have an answer beforehand, prepare yourself. Don't BS them, don't expose yourself by not knowing the right answer. It puts you in the position of being really weak because you feel like you're being not necessarily attacked, but when these questions come and you're not prepared for them, you don't feel as comfortable as you would if you prepared and knew the answer.

What will also happen is, let's say in the example about when the HVAC company, the air conditioning company was working with the landscaping company. When the landscaper had specific questions to the HVAC company about what his client was worth, how long they stayed with them, how many months they did business with them, if they did maintenance contracts. The HVAC company owner knew all the answers. He understood what the landscaping company owner was looking for. He knew that his answers were simply, "Well, we sell to our customers one time and then we typically don't do business with them for a long time." Now, I'm not saying that's the right or wrong answer for an HVAC company. All I'm saying is that's how his company did business. The answer went in even more depth. What he did say was that, "Well, as an AC contractor, once we install these units, we don't do a very good job of selling them maintenance contracts as you do in the landscaping business. You sell monthly contracts. Well, see that helped to reduce some of the risk to the buyer because the buyer didn't understand why in the world and HVAC contractor would only do a one-time sale and then never speak to a customer again, which just happens to be the way that this particular HVAC contractor did business.

He didn't have a very strong sales force, so he couldn't sell maintenance contracts very easily. It is not that his customers were not ready to buy, it's because he did a poor job at selling. That was one of his weaknesses. He knew that the landscaping contractor, who he had done his homework with, had a very strong sale force and could easily sell maintenance contracts to his customers because that's what they did. That's how the landscaping service worked, they did monthly contracts for mowing the lawn and coming and redoing the flower beds, and quarterly checking of the shrubbery, and trimming trees, and all that stuff. They were always involved with their customers.

It was something that was very easily talked about, easily connected with, and then as the conversation went on better questions could be asked about these topics such as:

- Well, how long do you think this sales process takes?
- What kind of customers do you have?
- What's their income level?
- Do they have large backyards that our landscaping could fit in with?

A lot more relevant questions, questions relevant to the growth of the landscaping contractors company. By being prepared, you're actually helping the other company to reach their goals, which in turn helps you get your a better price for any resources you need, which is exactly what you want anyway. When we're talking about negotiations and sales, when you're speaking with another company, you'll want to do a few things.

You'll want to take into consideration these few topics here. That each conversation, each communication you have with someone is results oriented. Now obviously it is, right? It's the whole reason to have a communication with them.

You want you to be comfortable with yourself, comfortable enough to be able to deal with someone asking you questions and not bring a lot of ego into this. You see, it's very easy for you to inflate the value of your customers, inflate your income, inflate what you think something is worth in your business. If someone can very easily come in and refute that evidence, we don't necessarily want to have that be a problem.

Take Ego Out of the Equation

What you'd rather you do is start asking yourself these questions from the buyer's perspective, come up with good answers, and not let your ego get into this. Make sure that these negotiations are results oriented and not ego oriented. Keep the focus on negotiation and the growth of your business, stay solely focused on the results that makes the best long-term value for both parties so that you both can have a great outcome of this. By taking the emphasis off the people.

Hell, you may not like the other person, you may be personally repulsed by this kind of a person you're negotiating with, but if the deal's there and the results are going to be achieved, it should not matter who this person is if he can afford to pay it, if he's going to do good things to help you grow your company. If you can both reach all your personal and financial objectives and goals, if you both take the personal side out and get rid of the ego and focus on the results, then you can both get all the best results you're looking for, just make sure that you are both being results oriented. You just want to make sure you understand that you're dealing with people when you're doing these negotiations, but don't let that get in the way with you being results oriented, and making sure that you achieve what you want to achieve.

Don't Take Things Personally

Another thing you want to make sure is that when you're doing these negotiations, be wise and not just smart about it. You'll want you to always show respect and understanding for the other party, and frame this negotiation, and especially the sales value around both of your interests rather than your interests alone. It makes it makes it easier for the other person to accept your offer or barter service if you're not just focusing in on your needs, if you're focusing in on their needs too. If you're respectful, you're more likely to have that be reciprocated to you if you're respectful. If you're an a-hole and be a butt head about your negotiations and have a bunch of snide comments, well that's exactly what the other person is going to do back to you. What goes around comes around, especially in negotiations.

Be Wise About the Big Picture

Don't take things too personal, don't let ego get into this, and not just being smart about this, that's going to serve you best when it comes to these negotiations.

Another thing you want to do is you want to make sure that the other company is much larger than you are and has more resources at their disposal than you do. That is one of the very first things you'll want to look for as an extraordinary resource.

Look for Someone With Many More Resources Than You Have

We want someone between 5 and 50 times the size of us. Well, that can sometimes be a little bit intimidating. When we're dealing with larger companies, we tend to want to do the things we've talked about. We tend to want to put ego in there, we tend to want to posture ourselves, we tend to want to exaggerate some of the results we achieve. Don't do that.

The best thing to do here is be completely honest, and even put your own concerns on the table. See, you being the smaller party in this negotiation, you might feel worried that the other company may not follow through with the deal, you think they may have more choices because they're the bigger company, you're the smaller company. I want you to know that that's not always true, and that if you simply voice your concerns on the front end such as, if you find out that maybe the other person thinks that your service can be replicated very easily without making a deal with your company.

In the case of the landscaping company getting help from the HVAC company, one of the questions that the HVAC company, had was, "Well, why wouldn't this landscaping company as large as they are simply hire some service techs and get a deal with a local AC manufacturer and start this kind of business on their own?" It was kind of a problem that the HVAC company had with himself. He wasn't as confident in what his company did, even though he did a great job.

What he did was instead of holding that in and thinking that at any time this much larger company could bury him and start a company on their own, he actually asked the buyer why they didn't do that. The buyer told him quite frankly, says, "You're absolutely right. We have that in our pocket. We could potentially do that but here's the reasons why we won't do that." He gave him a list. One of them was because he wanted to work with a company that had great customer value. He wanted to work with a company that already was well known within the industry, had some good will, already had the sound business practices, already had the relationships, and could help them to build their company a whole lot faster.

When you have concerns like this, instead of just keeping them to yourself and losing some confidence in this deal, which is so important to be confident about the value of your company and confident in these deals. Rather than keeping it to yourself, it's okay to bring this up to the other person at the appropriate time. As long as you're being honest and forthcoming, usually the other person will be that way with you, will give up some information in order to help the deal move forward.

Don't think that just because you're the smaller person in these deals that you have to posture yourself or that you have to keep all questions that you have, that you think are foolish or simple, that you don't need to have these questions answered. You do, and you do have a right to express these concerns and voice these problems even during negotiations. It doesn't put you in a weak position, it doesn't make you the weaker party to this negotiation. What it does is show that you are concerned about this, and it helps the other person to understand some of your needs as well. Because this entire topic we're talking here today is that you want to be familiar with both sides of the table, right? Well, so does the other person you are negotiating with.

The Resource Provider Should be Doing This Kind of Homework Too

He should be trying to figure out what your needs are as well. You reciprocate that by giving some of these needs on the front end. You actually tell him, "Hey, I have these issues." That helps them prepare on their end to make sure that they're prepared for this negotiation too, so you're doing them a favor by putting these concerns on the table. Just know that you're not putting yourself at a disadvantage by doing this, by voicing your concerns on the table.

Avoid the Use of "I"

Another thing you want to make sure that you do is that you avoid the word "I." It's going to come up, if you're doing this for yourself in your own life and in your business, but you'll want you to realize that if you can make this negotiation more about them, more about the buyer, you'll do yourself a huge service. This is a simple standard sales strategy is to be in the mindset of the other person so that you can sell your product. Not that you're going to be able to not use the word "I," but if you do that, you want to make sure that you avoid, "I want this and I want that, and I need this for this reason." If you can approach the subject and approach the other person with a "we" mentality or that, "Together, this can happen," you'll get a whole lot farther.

Just as you know when you're negotiating for anything that you're going to purchase, you should also know that the other person is all about them, they're really not looking out for you, and it breeds some distrust in the negotiation, and you understand that. Know that when you're doing this, you want to avoid making it all about you. That's the whole purpose of this entire process is to be aware of what's going on, on the other side of the table so that you can know what's happening and take the approach of that this is something that's good for both of you. Avoid the use of the word "I" if you can, and avoid the thought process that it's all about you when you're doing this.

Body Language is Important

This is a basic sales strategy here, but smiling is important as well as not leaning back when you're speaking to someone at a negotiation table. Leaning forward, putting your elbows on the table, looking at them in their eye, and engaging with them during these negotiations, and during these talks. You'll want you to make sure that you are engaged, and don't posture too much. Don't cross your arms, all that body language speaks a lot. Make sure you do make good eye contact, good handshakes. Use your body language appropriately so that you can convey the right message when you're speaking to the other person.

Good Table Manners Count

They're critical in negotiations, and not just making sure you don't put your elbows on the table. It's really about not having abusive behavior. If the other person gives you a little bit of grief about something or attacks you in some small way, avoid hitting back and giving them as good as they give it, back to you. Avoid that kind of mentality. Be in command of your behavior, particularly your emotional responses. If they hit you with some kind of question that takes you aback or either causes a little bit of embarrassment or cause a little bit of anger, what you'll want you to do is just take a few seconds, collect yourself, be in command of your own behavior, and don't let the negotiations destabilize because you're getting angry about some issue here.

Make This About the Issues

We talked about in the very beginning that this is all about results. Make this negotiation about the results and make it less about a personal attack. Even if you are attacked, be the bigger person. Be in control of this, be in command of your behavior. Don't fight back when they do attack you. Know that it takes two to play this game of fighting here. If they do it and you need a few seconds to calm down, that's fine. It's going to show a level of maturity, and I want you to refrain from responding in kind. Don't do what they did to you, that's not the way you want to play this game. Be the bigger person when it comes to manners in these negotiations and sales, and be the bigger person.

Avoid Negotiating Piecemeal

This means that when you prepare for your negotiations you will have lots and lots of questions and problems with the negotiated points. From price to delivery to quality, etc.. You will have a list of things that you'll want to cover with the other person about the fair exchange of value on both sides of the table. That is normal and perfectly acceptable. But what you will not want to do is to go through your list, line item by line item and put full negotiating into each and every line item. When you do this you both lose.

Instead of going line by line and negotiating every single line item and having give and take on every single line item, what you would rather you do instead of making lists of every single thing that you want is to take that list and go a step farther. Take that list and prioritize which one of those needs or wants or questions are most important to you. Get those items negotiated first, while leaving the large bulk of the simple things that you have questions or concerns about negotiated as a large bulk of issues.

You lose power as a buyer of services if you're going to do this in every single piece. What I want you to do is to say, let's just say for instance, for example that your service you offer to the other person is worth $10,000. If your company's service is worth $10,000 then you probably have 10 perfectly valid and different reasons why it's worth $10,000, and each one of those reasons is worth $1,000 to you. Don't go line by line and justify the reason why that one line item is worth $1,000. Because what you'll wind up doing is you'll wind up negotiating every single line item, and then adding all the line items up, and at the end of this you may have a lower amount.

Instead, what I would rather you do is to speak about each one of these line items and say as a whole, all ten of these reasons are worth $10,000. It will always, I don't want to say always, but in most cases it's going to come out better for you to negotiate as a whole the entire reasons rather than going line by line and negotiating these piecemeal. Now what I also want you to do is negotiate only when you know the needs of the other party.

You Need to Do Your Homework

The other person should do this as well, they should also do their homework on you as well. You'll want you to do even more to prepare. The only reason to negotiate is to produce a better outcome than you can get without negotiation. If you didn't have to negotiate, you just wanted to take whatever price they offered you, then don't negotiate at all. There's no reason to go into negotiations, there's no reason for you to start talking with the other person at all. If you accept their first offer, then there's no reason to do any of this.

The only point in negotiation is to get a better offer. To do that, you'll want you to do the homework you need to do. You need to be able to bridge the differences between the two of you in order for you to accommodate both parties, and structure good proposals and good final agreements. In order to do this, you have to know what the other guy needs, what the other guy wants. To do that, you got to do your homework.

Your homework is to go into your own company and prepare all those things, prepare answers and documents for all those answers to all those questions. Do your homework on the other person's company, know what their needs are. Know who it is that you have to contact about that, and start doing some of your own homework on there. We talked a little bit about being results oriented but you'll want you to make sure that you negotiate the problem and not the people.

You're Going to Be Dealing With People You May Not Like

You're going to be dealing with people who have differences of opinion, that don't agree with you on some items here, that don't agree with you on some of the points. Probably most of them you won't agree upon. Probably most of the things you speak about you won't agree with the price or the valuation. I want you to negotiate the problem and focus on the problem, and not necessarily just focus on the people that you're dealing with.

It's easy to get angry with somebody because they look different, act different, smell different, from a different part of the country, whatever it is, those things will get in the way if you want to make progress during these or any negotiations.

Negotiate the Problems

Usually the problems with valuation, problems with the business or numbers, those things can be resolved, and don't let the people actually get in the way. Have a great relationship. One way to do this is to have a great relationship with your buyer as best as possible. You can't always have a great relationship but what I want you to do is do things like try to talk friendly to somebody during breaks.

If you have a real structured negotiation where you're at the actual, physical negotiation table and you guys take a break, hey, it's okay to go grab a sandwich with him and have a little bit of friendly conversation, ask where they're from, how's their family doing? Those kinds of things ease the tension. Having a good relationship with the person you're negotiating against can act to your advantage.

Make Sure That They Have a Good Perception of You

It's easy in the heat of battle to view the person on the other side of the table as your enemy, to view them as someone that you're doing battle with and really trying to hurt and to take advantage of. The effective negotiators, they keep their cool, they get into the heads of the people they're doing business with or doing battle against, but they don't let that become an issue. They want to make sure that the other person thinks highly of them. You can do simple things like holding the door when someone wants to walk through it. Whatever gives you a better perception, gives them a better perception of you will help you.

Same thing with manners. We talked about that on the very beginning of this chapter here. Having great manners, having them have a high perception of you. Making sure that you don't show all those negative emotions when it comes down to it. If they make you angry, that those emotions don't come through in what you say or how you act. Don't throw your pen down or slam the book shut or whatever it is. If you get angry, handle yourself, be in control of your own emotions when you're going through these negotiations.

Even if they do have personal attacks that are against you, remember, you're negotiating this problem, you're not trying to negotiate with the people, so stick to the points that are relevant to these deals.

Communication, That's What This Is All About

All this negotiation, all this sales price, the entire process here is all about communication. It's all about getting your message into the head of the other person. It's all about making sure that the message you get into the buyer's head is the right message that helps you reach your personal and financial goals. Communicating that message to the other person is the entire reason for doing this entire negotiation process. The better you can do that, the more you can take from what we've talked about here today, the better off you'll be in the end.

This is all about great communication. One last thing I want to talk about is that while we spoke about negotiations between you and the other person is that this surface negotiation is not the only set of negotiations that are going on. All these things we mentioned here, yes, of course you want to do your homework, you want to have good manners, you want to have good communications with everyone, but there's also:

Negotiations Within the Negotiations

What that means is that within you and your own team. Within you and your lawyer, your CPA, your mastermind coach, maybe even your key employees. While you're going through this negotiation process, you know there are also going to be arguments and disagreements and differences of opinion amongst your own team between themselves and between you and them. If the other person values your business service one way and within your own team you simply can never agree that that value is accurate or inaccurate or whatever the problem may be, know that you want to apply all these same strategies and tactics within negotiations of your own team.

Not only does it apply when you're speaking to the person across the table, but have good manners, be in control of your emotions when you're speaking to your own people, when you're speaking to your own team. All this really plays a part in making sure that the negotiation on both sides of the table, whether it's from table side of the seller to the table side of the buyer, or within the seller's side of the table, when you're talking to all the people that are there to help you.

Make sure you use these negotiations, make sure that you understand everything that's gone on, on both sides of the discussions on your own side of the table, and you truly will have a much easier negotiation and get a much better results and in the long term help your business growth.

Growth Strategy Statement

The last part of this is to put together your massive growth strategy statement. What you'll want you to do now is to take the worksheets that you've completed and finish this massive growth strategy statement. You'll want you to put that someone, that who, that inner circle or outer circle member, that person showed you a strategy to, and then put down your idea. Put down your massive growth idea here. Such as "Bob showed you a strategy to put a board of directors in place", and then the next part of the statement is saying, "When I get," your extraordinary resource. Maybe your extraordinary resource is your board of directors and help from an extraordinary person, maybe it's the board of directors, your business will grow by whatever percent.

What you want you to do is put together your massive growth strategy statement, so that you can solidify this idea on paper, and show you exactly, exactly what it's going to take for you to achieve that massive growth number that you've got in step one. If your number of growth, your massive growth number you want to grow with was a 1,000%, so 10 times your size now, now you have a statement of a fact on exactly how to achieve that growth in your business. This is what those Inc. 5000 and Inc. 5000 members are doing to achieve that 1,700% growth in their business. (Buchanan, "What the Companies on the Inc. 5000 All Have in Common") This is exactly what the 99.99% of businesses are not doing, and that's why they're settling for mediocre growth. It's what we did and we settled for mediocre growth for a period of time, until we decided that we wanted massive growth. We had to have this massive growth strategy statement, what's included, what we're going to do, how we're going to do it, who we're going to do it with, and what our goal of growth was.

The only way to get to that goal is to have this statement, whether it's in your head or written down in this exercise. If nothing else, you'll want you to walk away from this book with this, walk away with this massive growth strategy statement, so that you know what it's going to take to grow your business in a huge way, and achieve your growth percentage. Now what you can do next is take that massive growth strategy statement, and whether you have it filled out or not, we can give you some specific help on making sure that you get this massive growth strategy statement done.

Chapter 9

Your Next Step Is Easier Than You Think

Your Best Next Step is Easier Than You Think

This process is not as hard as you think it is. Sure, we just gave you almost 200 pages of actions to take, but just as any long journey starts with the first step so does the path to massive business growth. The physical steps to take mean you'll need to sit at your desk and write some emails. You'll need to make a few phone calls and set up a few meetings. You'll need to have lunches with your colleagues and discuss strategies with other business owners. You may need to have a tough conversation or two during the negotiations and stand your ground when you make a decision. This is what this process is all about, but doesn't this resemble what you're doing now as the leader of your business. At some point in your career haven't you already done many of these activities? Of course you have, well then you'll just do them again but the topics and the goal will be to massively grow your business. This is new information to you and new strategies but it isn't rocket surgery or brain science.

The Right Questions

You of course will have a team, actually multiple teams working with you and for you to complete these actions and you will rely on their expertise. You simply have to know the right questions to go to your team with, then they will give you the answers and guide you through the strategic and tactical processes to complete whatever needs to be completed. You will need to know some specialized strategies so you can guide your team and allow them to help you do a little course correction but you are the captain and you steer the ship so you'll need to know where you are going and they'll help you get there.

Get Started Now

It takes time to grow a business massively so you'll need to get the process started now. Many business owners get discouraged when it comes time to grow, especially when they find out that it takes months and sometimes even years to get everything done.

Get A Guide

Big game hunters rarely just go hunting in an area all alone without first getting a guide to show them where to go, how to find the game and then how to make the final kill shot. So, just as a hunter would first find someone to help them with their hunt, so should you get someone to guide you in your hunt of big game to massively grow your company. Your guide should know the area well and have accomplished what it is you want to accomplish. You certainly can do it on your own but beware that you are playing with big game and it's likely that you'll get eaten alive without knowing what you are doing.

This Is What You Need To Do Now

If you've read to this point in the book you are undoubtedly motivated and driven to get to your own massive business growth. Whether you know who you're using to get your ideas from, let's say maybe you're inner and outer circle people didn't give you that ideas that will actually reach your massive growth strategy percentage. What you can do is, I'm going to give you access to what's called our jump start call, our massive growth jump start call. Go to www.TheDrivingForceBook.com, you'll see an application for you to simply write down your massive growth strategy statement or as close as you've got to it or if you don't have it done, you can check that box as well. But what you'll want you to do is schedule a call with one of our consultants that can give you help and get you this massive growth strategy statement done. Whether or not you have the idea or not, we can show you exactly, because we've done it so many times with our consultants, we can show you exactly what your massive growth strategy statement should be.

On this call, this massive growth jump start call, we're going to be able to be another member of your outer circle, if nothing else you can put that on your outer circle list. Put your massive growth jump start call, that will be on your outer circle list. If you don't know your massive growth idea, we're really good at coming up with those ideas, really good. Like within 45 minutes you'll have that idea in hand ready to go. We'll tell you what resources you need, as a matter of fact we're so good at facilitating these connections that we probably have that connection or that resource, that person that you need to connect to on our

Rolodex. Is the Rolodex even still around? There was a time when they were on every desk, but we will have them within our connections on our phones or wherever we keep all those contacts in. But we will probably have connections to the people and the resources you need right now to make your massive business growth idea come true.

Your massive growth jump start call is ultra-important, not only does it give you connections to someone that's outside your industry, we probably already have the resources and the people that you need to connect to, to get that one big idea to come true. What I want you to do right now is to go to www.TheDrivingForceBook.com, fill out the form, get your massive growth jump start call scheduled so that you can get your massive growth strategy statement completed and you can actually have everything that you need to grow your business in massive ways.

Chapter 10

Worksheets

Step 1 – Choose Massive Growth

What is your average year to year growth?

_____

What do you ideally want your growth to be next year?

_____

Step 2 – Find Your Massive Growth Idea

Inner Circle

1. Spouse
2. Board of Directors
3. Vice President
4. Family
5. Employees
6. Investors
7. Partners

Outer Circle

1. Business Owners – Competitors
2. Business Owners – Outside Your Industry
3. Coaches/Consultants/Masterminds
4. Your Vendors
5. Your CPA
6. Your Lawyer
7. Your Banker
8. Management Consultant

Top 10 Massive Idea Partners

Inner Circle

1. _____

2. _____

3. _____

4. _____

5. _____

Outer Circle

1. _____

2. _____

3. _____

4. _____

5. _____

You're Only One Idea Away From Massive Business Growth
Go to www.TheDrivingForceBook.com to get Your FREE Gift Worth $747.83

Idea Generator

New/Customer/Client Ideas

Existing Customer/Client Ideas

Increase Sales for Your Company

Reduce Costs for Your Company

Technology

Changing Packaging

Better Sales Processes

Better Sales Capabilities

Better Marketing Processes

Better Marketing Capabilities

Adding New Services

Economies of Scale – Better Pricing

Incorporating New Components/Services In the Product

More Product Options

Changing the Marketing Message

Increasing Marketing Channels

Sources for Important Resources

Connections with other people

Leadership

1. How can my Massive Idea Partner's Leadership system improve my product or service and make them more valuable?

   _____
   _____

2. How can my Massive Idea Partner's Leadership system or skills or resources make my customer or clients more valuable?

   _____
   _____

3. Massive Idea Partner's Leadership system or skills or resources give my business a brand-new product or service?

   _____
   _____

4. Massive Idea Partner's Leadership system or skills or resources give me a new customer or client?

   _____
   _____

Management

5. How can my Massive Idea Partner's Management system improve my product or service and make them more valuable?

   _____

   _____

6. How can my Massive Idea Partner's Management system or skills or resources make my customer or clients more valuable?

   _____

   _____

7. Massive Idea Partner's Management system or skills or resources give my business a brand-new product or service?

   _____

   _____

8. Massive Idea Partner's Management system or skills or resources give me a new customer or client?

   _____

   _____

The Driving Force Massive
Business Growth Formula

Financial

9. How can my Massive Idea Partner's Financial system improve my product or service and make them more valuable?

_____
_____

10. How can my Massive Idea Partner's Financial system or skills or resources make my customer or clients more valuable?

_____
_____

11. Massive Idea Partner's Financial system or skills or resources give my business a brand-new product or service?

_____
_____

12. Massive Idea Partner's Financial system or skills or resources give me a new customer or client?

_____
_____

You're Only One Idea Away From Massive Business Growth
Go to www.TheDrivingForceBook.com to get Your FREE Gift Worth $747.83

Marketing

13. How can my Massive Idea Partner's Marketing system improve my product or service and make them more valuable?

　_____

　_____

14. How can my Massive Idea Partner's Marketing system or skills or resources make my customer or clients more valuable?

　_____

　_____

15. Massive Idea Partner's Marketing system or skills or resources give my business a brand-new product or service?

　_____

　_____

16. Massive Idea Partner's Marketing system or skills or resources give me a new customer or client?

　_____

　_____

Sales

17. How can my Massive Idea Partner's Sales system improve my product or service and make them more valuable?

_____
_____

18. How can my Massive Idea Partner's Sales system or skills or resources make my customer or clients more valuable?

_____
_____

19. Massive Idea Partner's Sales system or skills or resources give my business a brand-new product or service?

_____
_____

20. Massive Idea Partner's Sales system or skills or resources give me a new customer or client?

_____
_____

Production

21. How can my Massive Idea Partner's Production system improve my product or service and make them more valuable?

   _____
   _____

22. How can my Massive Idea Partner's Production system or skills or resources make my customer or clients more valuable?

   _____
   _____

23. Massive Idea Partner's Production system or skills or resources give my business a brand-new product or service?

   _____
   _____

24. Massive Idea Partner's Production system or skills or resources give me a new customer or client?

   _____
   _____

The Driving Force Massive
Business Growth Formula

Putting It All Together

25. Now take all of your ideas and summarize your Massive Growth Idea and all of the parts of your business that you'll need to put it together to make sure that it will happen as quickly as possible.

_____
_____
_____
_____
_____
_____
_____
_____
_____
_____

You're Only One Idea Away From Massive Business Growth
Go to www.TheDrivingForceBook.com to get Your FREE Gift Worth $747.83

Step 3 – Massive Action Mode
To set up your massive action work environment:

- ✓ Find a quiet room where you won't be disturbed
- ✓ Put a Do Not Disturb sign on the door, then close it and lock it
- ✓ Put phone on do not disturb or just unplug it
- ✓ Turn off you cell phone
- ✓ Turn off your email
- ✓ Turn off any instant messaging or chat features
- ✓ Close out of all programs except the one you are using to complete this exercise

Step 4 – Connect To Extraordinary People

Who can make more money than you can from your products?

_____
_____
_____

Who can remove a constraint on your business?

_____
_____
_____

Who has a problem you can fix?

_____
_____
_____

What threat can you reduce or eliminate?

_____
_____
_____

Who sells to the same customers you sell to?

_____

_____

_____

Who uses the same technology you use?

_____

_____

_____

Who needs your customer base?

_____

_____

_____

Who needs your technology or people?

_____

_____

_____

Step 5 - The Resources You're Going To Need

1. **Money** – How much will you need? When will you need it?

   _____
   _____
   _____

2. **Lists** – Will you need more leads to feed into your marketing and sales funnel? Who are they? How many lists of leads will you possibly need? Give details here.

   _____
   _____
   _____

3. **Outsourcing** – Can you turn over specific functions to a third party provider to implement and support, for a fee?

   _____
   _____
   _____

4. **Joint Ventures** – Do you need any strategic alliances where two or more parties form a partnership to share markets, assets, knowledge, and, of course, profits?

_____
_____
_____

5. **Affiliates** – Do you need a type of re-seller arrangement where the affiliate refers customers and is rewarded financially for doing so?

_____
_____
_____

6. **Technology** – Do you need to use other people's technology to cut overheads, streamline operations, access new markets, support remote workers etc?

_____
_____
_____

The Driving Force Massive
Business Growth Formula

7. **Systems** – Will you need new systematizing of any of your business functions so that they operate with the least amount of human intervention?

_____
_____
_____

8. **Exchanging Services** – You will need to be able to barter your services with those of another person or company for mutual benefit. This will reduce the amount of money you may need. Which services can you use for bartering to reach your massive idea?

_____
_____
_____

9. **Mastermind Groups** – You will need to regularly connect with and exploit the talents, contacts, ideas, experience, intelligence etc. of like-minded peers. Which groups will you be a part of?

_____
_____
_____

10. **Other** – What other needs do you feel will be absolutely crucial to achieve your Massive Growth Idea?

_____

_____

_____

NOTES:

Biery, Mary Ellen. (Contributor) "The State Of U.S. Small Businesses Entering 2016." *Forbes,* 17 Jan. 2016. 18 Sep. 2017. https://www.forbes.com/sites/sageworks/2016/01/17/the-state-of-u-s-small-businesses-entering-2016

Buchanan, Leigh. (Ed.) "What the Companies on the Inc. 5000 All Have in Common." *Inc.* Sep. 2015. 18 Sep. 2017. https://www.inc.com/magazine/201509/leigh-buchanan/2015-inc5000-how-to-rocket-up-the-learning-curve.html

Made in the USA
Middletown, DE
06 December 2018